XLB 2047
© 1987 Loveline Publishing Ltd, London, England.
Printed and bound in Italy.
ISBN 0 86283 679 4

The Illustrated
KAMA SUTRA

Loveline Books

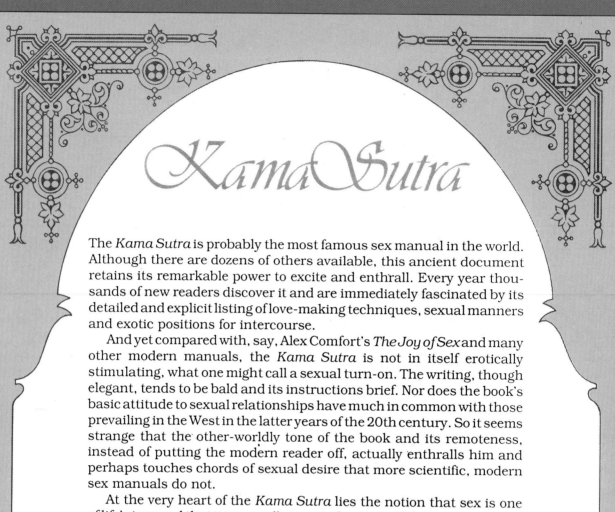

Kama Sutra

The *Kama Sutra* is probably the most famous sex manual in the world. Although there are dozens of others available, this ancient document retains its remarkable power to excite and enthrall. Every year thousands of new readers discover it and are immediately fascinated by its detailed and explicit listing of love-making techniques, sexual manners and exotic positions for intercourse.

And yet compared with, say, Alex Comfort's *The Joy of Sex* and many other modern manuals, the *Kama Sutra* is not in itself erotically stimulating, what one might call a sexual turn-on. The writing, though elegant, tends to be bald and its instructions brief. Nor does the book's basic attitude to sexual relationships have much in common with those prevailing in the West in the latter years of the 20th century. So it seems strange that the other-worldly tone of the book and its remoteness, instead of putting the modern reader off, actually enthralls him and perhaps touches chords of sexual desire that more scientific, modern sex manuals do not.

At the very heart of the *Kama Sutra* lies the notion that sex is one of life's joys and that it is actually a part of everyday living, to be spoken, sung, danced and thought about; to be discussed openly and to be taught as a social skill alongside reading, writing and conversation.

During the last twenty years or so, sex is generally supposed to have come out of the closet in the West. We pride ourselves on our openness about it and can point to the million-dollar industry it has created. But in many important ways, we still show a tendency to regard our sex lives and activities as being separate from ordinary day-by-day living, not as an integral part of 'real life'. In our private lives sex is confined to the bedroom (often a dark one), is not spoken of in front of the children (or older people either) and so is kept as a kind of secret to be shared only at crisis points with a doctor or, if things get really tough, with a sex therapist. In public life sex has become part of the entertainment industry through books, magazines, films and 'special' clubs, whether of the conventional 'strip club' variety or catering for more specialist interests. And all this is available in separate, clearly-defined sections of our cities and always surrounded by warning signs – red lights, 'adults only' slogans and heavily screened windows.

This kind of attitude is quite alien to the *Kama Sutra*. The book

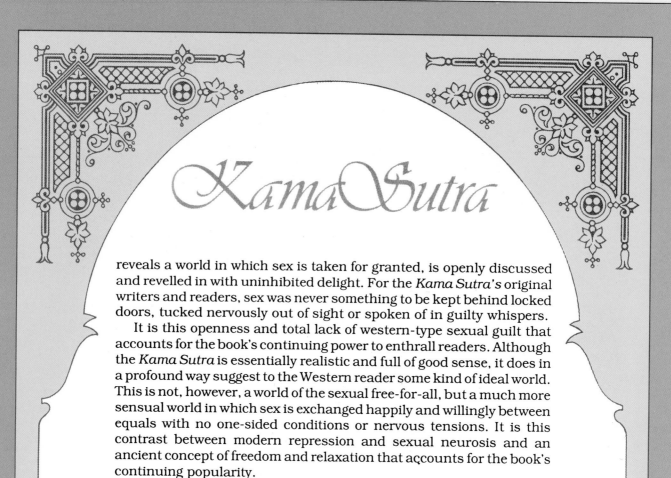

Kama Sutra

reveals a world in which sex is taken for granted, is openly discussed and revelled in with uninhibited delight. For the *Kama Sutra's* original writers and readers, sex was never something to be kept behind locked doors, tucked nervously out of sight or spoken of in guilty whispers.

It is this openness and total lack of western-type sexual guilt that accounts for the book's continuing power to enthrall readers. Although the *Kama Sutra* is essentially realistic and full of good sense, it does in a profound way suggest to the Western reader some kind of ideal world. This is not, however, a world of the sexual free-for-all, but a much more sensual world in which sex is exchanged happily and willingly between equals with no one-sided conditions or nervous tensions. It is this contrast between modern repression and sexual neurosis and an ancient concept of freedom and relaxation that accounts for the book's continuing popularity.

At this stage one example will suffice. The *Kama Sutra* has a section on what we might call 'group sex' – that is, one man enjoying two women or several women at the same time, or several men enjoying one woman at the same time. The sexual codes of our age stress monogamy as the ideal, and also assert the supremacy of one-to-one love relationships. This passage in the *Kama Sutra* then possibly represents to many men a kind of unattainable fantasy – something which would be almost impossible to achieve with friends, but which might just possibly be bought. Some might see it as downright immoral or actually perverted.

In the context of the *Kama Sutra*, however this kind of pleasure can be interpreted as a delightful fact of social life. And it is underpinned by a kind of moral code – different from those to which we ascribe, but a moral code nonetheless. Love, respect and consent are part of it, but the status and sometimes relationships of the participants are important too. A woman to be enjoyed by several men should be married to one of them. The two women enjoyed by one man should 'love him equally' and so on. The social status of the *Kama Sutra's* original audience is important to an understanding of the entire book and will be briefly discussed later.

Apart from its famous descriptions of positions for sexual intercourse, the *Kama Sutra* also contains a considerable amount of related sexual information, some of which is as valid today as it was when it

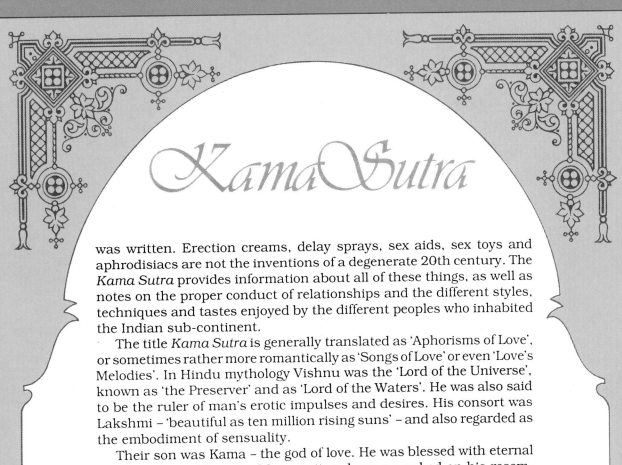

Kama Sutra

was written. Erection creams, delay sprays, sex aids, sex toys and aphrodisiacs are not the inventions of a degenerate 20th century. The *Kama Sutra* provides information about all of these things, as well as notes on the proper conduct of relationships and the different styles, techniques and tastes enjoyed by the different peoples who inhabited the Indian sub-continent.

The title *Kama Sutra* is generally translated as 'Aphorisms of Love', or sometimes rather more romantically as 'Songs of Love' or even 'Love's Melodies'. In Hindu mythology Vishnu was the 'Lord of the Universe', known as 'the Preserver' and as 'Lord of the Waters'. He was also said to be the ruler of man's erotic impulses and desires. His consort was Lakshmi – 'beautiful as ten million rising suns' – and also regarded as the embodiment of sensuality.

Their son was Kama – the god of love. He was blessed with eternal youth and great beauty. Many writers have remarked on his resemblance to Cupid, since Kama also shoots arrows from a bow. His arrows are made from flowers and his bow is constructed from flowers and bees. Kama rides on a dove and is particularly associated with springtime. All this seems very similar to our own myths of love, springtime, the birds and the bees. Kama was believed to hover, invisibly, over all acts of love. His wife was Rati, regarded as the embodiment of sensual love.

It is impossible to say precisely when Kama's songs of love were first written down. The nearest Sanskrit scholars can get is to place the work somewhere between the first and fourth centuries A.D. So it is between 1,900 and 1,600 years old. Its author is always referred to as Vatsyayana, though his own name was Mallanaga. But since he belonged to the Vatsyayana sect he is known by that name. As its title tells us, the book is written in sutra form – that is in aphorisms: short, pithy sentences using the minimum of words. It is this rather stark, uncoloured and unemotional style that makes the *Kama Sutra* initially off-putting for the modern mind. We tend to demand and expect more detail, more explanation, more heightened description. But it was, at that time, the traditional and accepted way of writing down with brevity what were in fact very complicated and involved philosophic systems. The highly detailed system of yoga, for example, is condensed into the *Patanjali*

Kama Sutra

Sutra.

The main reason why important philosophical texts were written in this form seems to have been to make them easier for students and others to remember, especially at a time when written material was not widely available. This implies, of course, that there must have been in existence lengthy and detailed commentaries on the various *Sutras* which would explain and elaborate on the bare sentences. Scholars argue that, since the *Kama Sutra* had achieved an authoritative position in Hindu philosophical literature at least by the 4th century, then there must have been several extended commentaries written. But none of these has survived.

Throughout the following centuries this pre-eminence remained unchallenged. Vatsyayana's work was regarded as the standard treatise on love in Sanskrit literature and copies were closely guarded in libraries all over the sub-continent. The first English translation of the *Kama Sutra* was the result of comparing copies from the libraries of Bombay, Benares, Calcutta and Jaipur.

This translation was first printed in 1883. It was beautifully produced, but anonymously, for 'the Kama Shastra Society of London and Benares, and for private circulation only'. Behind the project were two men: Sir Richard Burton, the charismatic and eminent Orientalist, linguist and explorer, and his long-standing friend and colleague, a retired Indian civil servant called Forster Fitzgerald Arbuthnot. Also involved, in the role of background patron, was Richard Monckton Miles, who had a passion for erotica.

Burton and Arbuthnot together created the Kama Shastra Society and between 1883 and 1888 published five classics or Oriental erotica, including the *Ananga Ranga* and the Arab classic *The Perfumed Garden*. Burton was also celebrated for his complete and unabridged translation of the *Arabian Nights*, which in its original form has little or no resemblance to the watered-down pantomime texts we are familiar with. The Italian director Pasolini's film *A Thousand and One Nights* captures quite a lot of the erotic nature of this work.

A modern cynic, looking back over more than a hundred years, might decide that Arbuthnot and Burton were just a couple of Victorian pornographers with their handsomely bound, privately circulated

Kama Sutra

Oriental sex books. But this was far from the case. Although at that time the flag of the British Empire flew strongly over India, very little was known about the culture or literature of the country. Both men knew that in order to understand an alien culture it was important to understand how the people lived – and this, of course, included their attitudes to and understanding of sex, love and personal relationships. This was the main stimulus for this publishing venture, and from the start the *Kama Sutra* aroused great interest. It was pirated in India itself, and in 1885 translated into French, following which its importance regarding research into Indian history and culture was quickly recognised. It is possible, however, that Arbuthnot has another motive for his participation. A sensitive man, he seems to have recognised that Victorian society was plagued with sexual ignorance, that the average man treated the average woman badly, that a total lack of knowledge about the basic intimacies of life was responsible for much unhappiness. The *Kama Sutra* he felt, with its explicit instructions about love-making and with its loving and responsible attitude to women, might in some way make a dent in this ignorance.

Today, it seems absurd to recommend the book as a kind of marriage manual for the late Victorians, but the information it contained, while most certainly raising a few eyebrows, might also have opened a few eyes in much the same way that the books of sexual instruction produced today have done.

As the 20th century dawned, the *Kama Sutra's* role as a sex manual was quickly superseded, but it remains arguably the first production in a long and worthwhile tradition. The image of a staid Victorian couple attempting to reproduce the positions designed for a much more relaxed and flexible people may strike us as amusing, but at least they were able to understand that the missionary position was not the beginning and end of all sexual intercourse. The *Kama Sutra* has been translated several times since Burton's initial attempt – but probably never so well – and today it ranks as one of the world's great classics of erotic literature.

Kama Sutra

An Erotic Lifestyle

Anybody picking up the *Kama Sutra* and expecting a highly-charged 'pornographic' read is bound to be disappointed. The section which deals with sexual union is substantial, detailed and explicit and, when read carefully, is extremely erotic. But this is only one section of a fairly long treatise. Vatsyayana is, in fact, dealing with the whole area of love, relationships, lifestyle and the proper conduct of his readers.

However, all this other material is pervaded with an acute sexual and sensual awareness which can be best appreciated if one understands a little of the Hindu attitude to the good life, and to sex in particular. To the Hindu, the good, or complete, life meant that the individual must attempt to achieve harmony between three essential activities. These are *Dharma*, which means a life of religious obligation; *Artha*, which refers to economic and political activity, and *Kama*, which is the life of the senses.

One of the fundamental differences between this view of life and that which prevails in the late 20th century relates to this aspiration to harmony. This difference occurs quite frequently. In this context, for example, we are used to the idea of the high-powered businessman who devotes his life to making money and Wall Street achievement, but whose personal and emotional life is empty. We might also recognise the character for whom the pursuit of sensual pleasures (sex, drugs and rock 'n' roll) is paramount and who ends as a burned-out wreck in early middle-age.

And then there are those women and men who decide to commit their lives to religious pursuits and who reject both the world of careerism and money-making and the world of passion and sexual gratification.

The Hindu philosophy recognised the importance of all three strands, but insisted they should be studied and practised equally so that the happy person achieved an appropriate blend of all three. In both philosophical writings and in popular works of the imagination (poems, plays, stories) the importance of this balance was always emphasised; pursuing two of the essential activities and neglecting the third (whichever it may have been) was always discouraged.

Kama Sutra

From this brief explanation then, it can be seen that the *Kama Sutra* was not just a sex book (pillow book, marriage manual or erotic diversion) as it has tended to become regarded in the West. It was an important statement about what was recognised as an integral part of life. Even to call it a book about 'sex' underestimates it. It is, in fact, a book about the life of the senses.

The intellectual rigour of this approach can quite easily be seen over and over again in Vatsyayana's writing. Throughout the book, at what would be controversial points, he pre-empts his possible critics and answers them. He tackles one of these right at the beginning, when he defends his stance that *Kama* should be studied like any other science.

His critics, he suggests, will say that since *Dharma* involves philosophical debate and intellectual thought then it is appropriate as the subject of a book. *Kama*, however, is natural both to humans and to animals, it is an instinct which needs no intellectual discussion when you can see it everywhere.

This argument is, of course, one that has cropped up many times during the 'sexual revolution' of the last quarter of a century. Sex is a natural instinct, say the moralists, which everybody can do naturally. To produce sex manuals, full of physical and clinical detail and instructions for love-making, reduces it all to a matter of heartless technology, removes the mystery and emotion.

To his critics, the author of the *Kama Sutra* replied that this was just not so. After all, he argued, sexual intercourse involves men and women who have a great deal more about them than the animals (who may indeed 'do it naturally'). If people learn the proper means from the *Kama Sutra*, and this involves a sense of responsibility, then their lives will be happier.

This is not unlike the answers given to modern critics. There is a great difference between 'doing it naturally' and 'doing it properly'. The 'natural' swimmer, for example, may be able to get himself across the lake well enough – but at great expense of energy, waste of movement and breath. The swimmer who has bothered to learn style and technique will also get across the lake, but with more speed, elegance and a greater sense of physical achievement. So it is with sex. A man may know 'instinctively' what to do in bed, but it will amount to little

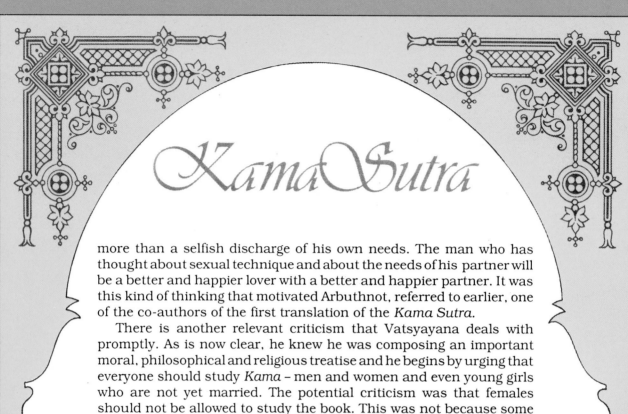

Kama Sutra

more than a selfish discharge of his own needs. The man who has thought about sexual technique and about the needs of his partner will be a better and happier lover with a better and happier partner. It was this kind of thinking that motivated Arbuthnot, referred to earlier, one of the co-authors of the first translation of the *Kama Sutra*.

There is another relevant criticism that Vatsyayana deals with promptly. As is now clear, he knew he was composing an important moral, philosophical and religious treatise and he begins by urging that everyone should study *Kama* – men and women and even young girls who are not yet married. The potential criticism was that females should not be allowed to study the book. This was not because some moralists would feel that it was too strong for girls, or that women should be kept ignorant of sex and sexual practise, but because females generally were not allowed, at that time, to study sciences, which were regarded as the exclusive domain of men.

Vatsyayana comes back smartly and realistically by pointing out that women know about it anyway, in much the same way that people who are ignorant of the details of grammar are still able to communicate correctly with each other. So why deny women the opportunity for greater knowledge? He goes on to urge that before she is married a girl's teachers (or studying companions) should include a trusted and older married woman. After marriage all she required was her husband's consent.

This reservation about women and girls being allowed to study a 'science' involved rather more than just the arts of love. In the *Kama Sutra* no particular distinction is made between the words 'art' and 'science' – they seem interchangeable. Along with sexual knowledge and expertise the *Kama Sutra* lists 64 arts which should be studied. These comprise what was known as the *Kama Shastra* – that is, the doctrines of love, a term which embraces the whole of the life of the senses.

Both men and women are urged to study, and perfect, as many of the 64 arts as they could – and any person who achieved this would most certainly have been seen as someone of wide-ranging ability. Even though several of these arts do seem more appropriate to men than to women, and vice versa, that everyone was urged to study them does

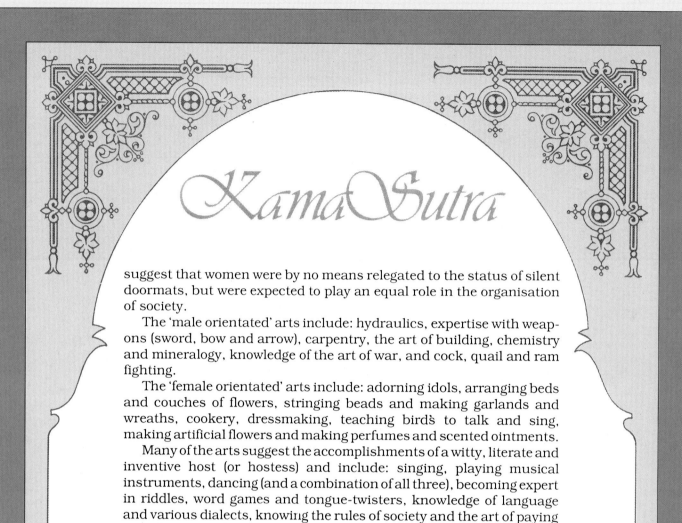

Kama Sutra

suggest that women were by no means relegated to the status of silent doormats, but were expected to play an equal role in the organisation of society.

The 'male orientated' arts include: hydraulics, expertise with weapons (sword, bow and arrow), carpentry, the art of building, chemistry and mineralogy, knowledge of the art of war, and cock, quail and ram fighting.

The 'female orientated' arts include: adorning idols, arranging beds and couches of flowers, stringing beads and making garlands and wreaths, cookery, dressmaking, teaching bird's to talk and sing, making artificial flowers and making perfumes and scented ointments.

Many of the arts suggest the accomplishments of a witty, literate and inventive host (or hostess) and include: singing, playing musical instruments, dancing (and a combination of all three), becoming expert in riddles, word games and tongue-twisters, knowledge of language and various dialects, knowing the rules of society and the art of paying compliments, playing charades, expertise in sports and fluency in conversation.

And yet others, while apparently concerned mainly with personal appearance and hygiene, do have, as we shall see later, a specifically sexual function: tattooing, colouring the nails, hair and features, proper disposition of personal jewellery and adornments, creating interesting kinds of drinks – and working with magic or sorcery!

It is quite a list of accomplishments. If one were making up such a list in today's terms one would want to add such skills as driving, piloting, computer technology, photography and several of the more adventurous sports. But to find a person these days with such all-round abilities would be rare. Perhaps the only comparatively modern equivalent is the young European woman of the 19th century who was expected to master a great many skills, from supervising a large household, to painting, singing, playing an instrument, knowing first aid and having a wide knowledge of literature and poetry. Today we tend to specialize or, some would say, restrict ourselves to one or two particular abilities which have a personal appeal.

But, following the doctrines of *Kama*, the 64 arts were not just diversions to keep idle people busy, they were intended to expand

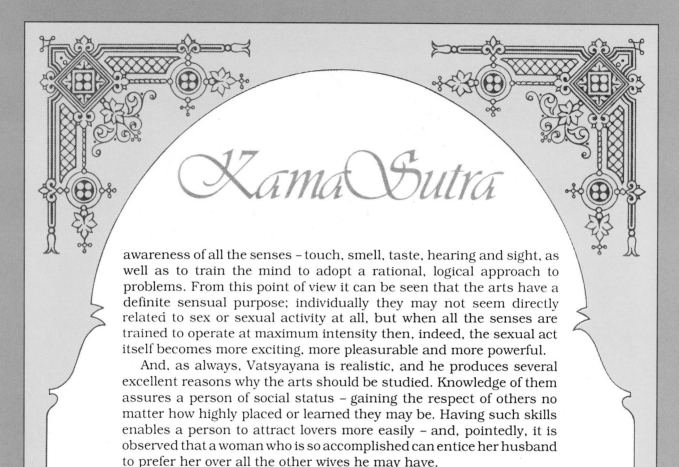

Kama Sutra

awareness of all the senses – touch, smell, taste, hearing and sight, as well as to train the mind to adopt a rational, logical approach to problems. From this point of view it can be seen that the arts have a definite sensual purpose; individually they may not seem directly related to sex or sexual activity at all, but when all the senses are trained to operate at maximum intensity then, indeed, the sexual act itself becomes more exciting, more pleasurable and more powerful.

And, as always, Vatsyayana is realistic, and he produces several excellent reasons why the arts should be studied. Knowledge of them assures a person of social status – gaining the respect of others no matter how highly placed or learned they may be. Having such skills enables a person to attract lovers more easily – and, pointedly, it is observed that a woman who is so accomplished can entice her husband to prefer her over all the other wives he may have.

An unmarried person – or a woman who has been separated from her husband – will find it easier to be self-supporting if she has as many of the 64 arts as possible at her fingertips. In this section Vatsyayana acknowledges that, both for men and for women, personal charm is always important in the development of social and romantic relationships, but the essential message is that mastery of these arts represents a certain path to personal, social and, above all, sexual success.

The concept of sex as an art form, and one that should be studied as much by women as by men, is one of the most powerful themes of the *Kama Sutra*, and related to this is the attitude it reveals towards women. Hindu society at the time was highly organised and well-regulated, but within these rules women enjoyed a remarkable amount of freedom and autonomy. It would be pointless to try and suggest that sexual and personal relationships were in any way based on the idea of total equality between the sexes, but it is evident that, in other cultures and in other centuries, women have had far rougher deals. It was the sense of respect and tenderness towards women that touched many of the Victorian readers of the first translation of the book. When the writer turns to practical sex instructions he does, as we shall see, maintain this attitude, especially in relation to foreplay, courting and the aftermath of love.

The rules of the erotic lifestyle are clearly detailed in the opening

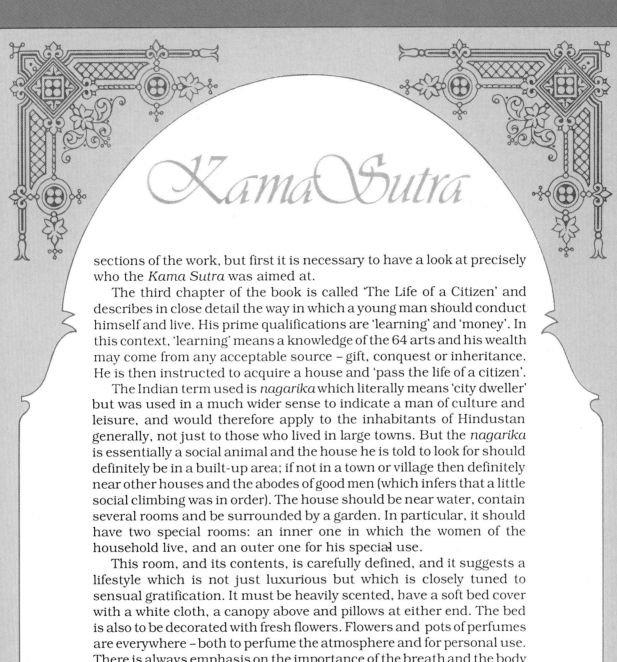

Kama Sutra

sections of the work, but first it is necessary to have a look at precisely who the *Kama Sutra* was aimed at.

The third chapter of the book is called 'The Life of a Citizen' and describes in close detail the way in which a young man should conduct himself and live. His prime qualifications are 'learning' and 'money'. In this context, 'learning' means a knowledge of the 64 arts and his wealth may come from any acceptable source – gift, conquest or inheritance. He is then instructed to acquire a house and 'pass the life of a citizen'.

The Indian term used is *nagarika* which literally means 'city dweller' but was used in a much wider sense to indicate a man of culture and leisure, and would therefore apply to the inhabitants of Hindustan generally, not just to those who lived in large towns. But the *nagarika* is essentially a social animal and the house he is told to look for should definitely be in a built-up area; if not in a town or village then definitely near other houses and the abodes of good men (which infers that a little social climbing was in order). The house should be near water, contain several rooms and be surrounded by a garden. In particular, it should have two special rooms: an inner one in which the women of the household live, and an outer one for his special use.

This room, and its contents, is carefully defined, and it suggests a lifestyle which is not just luxurious but which is closely tuned to sensual gratification. It must be heavily scented, have a soft bed cover with a white cloth, a canopy above and pillows at either end. The bed is also to be decorated with fresh flowers. Flowers and pots of perfumes are everywhere – both to perfume the atmosphere and for personal use. There is always emphasis on the importance of the breath and the body smelling sweetly.

There should be a box or casket for his jewellery and personal ornaments, a board for practising drawing, some books, a dice and board, other games and toys. His musical instrument should hang there, too. Outside in the garden are caged birds, a pair of swings and a flower-bedecked bower for sitting in.

A daily routine is also outlined. His first duty on rising is to wash his teeth and perfume and oil his body in moderation. He must put on a few ornaments and colour his eyes and lips – makeup served a functional purpose in that it protected the sensitive lips and eyelids

Kama Sutra

from the direct heat of the sun. He is instructed to chew betel leaves to make his breath pleasant and give himself a final once-over in the looking glass before going about his usual business.

The *nagarika* was expected to bathe daily and to oil himself all over every second day. His face and head were to be shaved every four days and the other parts of his body every week. He must also pay careful attention to removing the sweat from his armpits.

He eats three meals a day and in the mornings he divides his time between training his birds to talk, training cocks and rams for fighting and enjoying light conversation with friends. Then he is allowed a midday siesta during the summer months. After this he dresses again (perhaps more elaborately) and goes out to meet people and possibly to conduct business.

The evening are devoted to romance. After dinner there is singing and then he awaits the arrival of the woman who is attached to him in the room which has been freshly tidied, decorated and perfumed. He can send a female messenger for the woman or he can collect her himself. She is welcomed and entertained with 'loving and agreeable' conversation. That is the programme for a typical day, but the *Kama Sutra* also lists appropriate diversions or amusements that may be done occasionally. These include attending religious festivals, enjoying social gatherings of both sexes, hosting drinks parties and organising picnics.

The social gatherings – composed of equals (men of the same age, talents and tastes) – seem to have been quite serious-minded affairs involving the writing of verses and conversation about the arts. At the drinking parties it is interesting to note that the women were expected to drink first and only then were the men allowed to. Picnic entertainments included cock fighting and sometimes mixed bathing. The participants would wend their way home exhausted at the end of the day, bearing armfuls of flowers.

It would be extremely difficult to find anyone enjoying a comparable lifestyle today. A superficial reading does make it sound as if the *nagarika* was leisured, wealthy and indolent – and no doubt there are similar individuals around like that now. But to find a whole community or nation living in this idyllic style seems unlikely. It should,

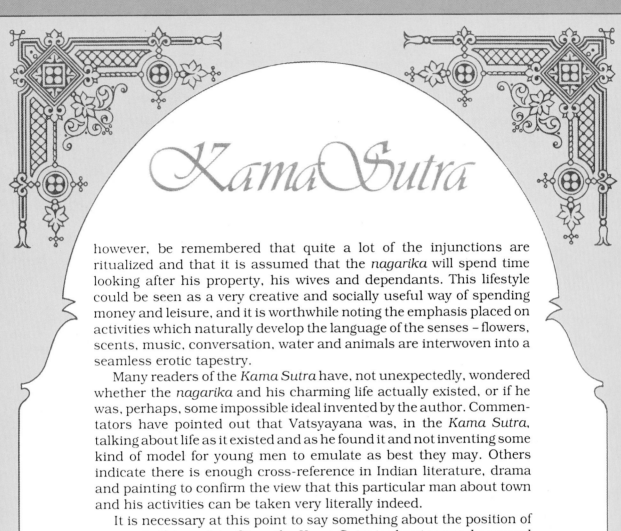

Kama Sutra

however, be remembered that quite a lot of the injunctions are ritualized and that it is assumed that the *nagarika* will spend time looking after his property, his wives and dependants. This lifestyle could be seen as a very creative and socially useful way of spending money and leisure, and it is worthwhile noting the emphasis placed on activities which naturally develop the language of the senses – flowers, scents, music, conversation, water and animals are interwoven into a seamless erotic tapestry.

Many readers of the *Kama Sutra* have, not unexpectedly, wondered whether the *nagarika* and his charming life actually existed, or if he was, perhaps, some impossible ideal invented by the author. Commentators have pointed out that Vatsyayana was, in the *Kama Sutra*, talking about life as it existed and as he found it and not inventing some kind of model for young men to emulate as best they may. Others indicate there is enough cross-reference in Indian literature, drama and painting to confirm the view that this particular man about town and his activities can be taken very literally indeed.

It is necessary at this point to say something about the position of women in this society. Since the *Kama Sutra* is about sex and personal relationships, its author is, of course, concerned only with the kinds of women who are appropriate partners for the *nagarika*. And he makes a clear distinction between two categories of women – wives and 'public women'. His attitude to marriage and to the wife is orthodox and conventional – even in today's terms. A suitable wife is essential for both the well-being and social status of the householder: she provides children, comfort, stability and reputation. Her role is to sustain the household (in which there might well be many other women), to organise the garden, the housekeeping and the food and never to do anything without the agreement of her husband. She keeps what today we might call a low profile, shunning dubious characters (such as fortune tellers and beggars), and avoiding over-dressing or over-decorating herself – but always making sure she looks really good when she presents herself to her husband.

This may look like a recipe for female submission to the arrogant male. But the wife did have a certain amount of autonomy, and if her husband followed the instructions given in the *Kama Sutra* she would

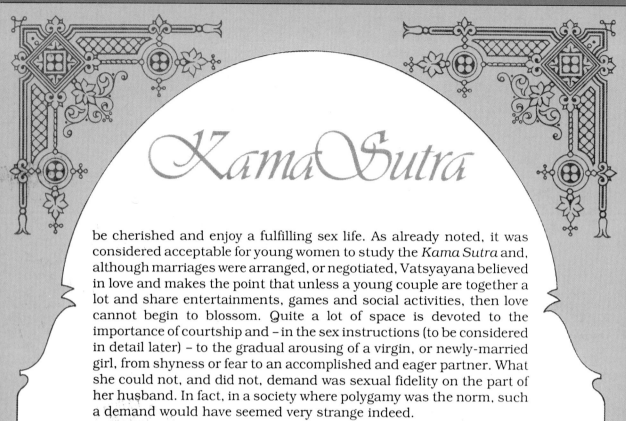

Kama Sutra

be cherished and enjoy a fulfilling sex life. As already noted, it was considered acceptable for young women to study the *Kama Sutra* and, although marriages were arranged, or negotiated, Vatsyayana believed in love and makes the point that unless a young couple are together a lot and share entertainments, games and social activities, then love cannot begin to blossom. Quite a lot of space is devoted to the importance of courtship and – in the sex instructions (to be considered in detail later) – to the gradual arousing of a virgin, or newly-married girl, from shyness or fear to an accomplished and eager partner. What she could not, and did not, demand was sexual fidelity on the part of her husband. In fact, in a society where polygamy was the norm, such a demand would have seemed very strange indeed.

Orthodox Western teaching on sex and marriage insists on monogamy and fidelity. More importantly, it insists that the true purpose of sexual intercourse is the production of children. Sometimes it is grudgingly admitted that sex can be a pleasurable activity, but only if it is kept within the monogamous parameters. The *Kama Sutra* takes a slightly different view and takes it for granted that sex is for pleasure as well as for progeny. And this means that men will seek variety, different experiences, different women.

There were four categories of women available for the sex-for-pleasure principle: women of lower caste than the *nagarika*, women who had been rejected from their own class, women who had been married twice, and the 'public' women, or courtesans.

There is a whole section of the *Kama Sutra* devoted to the manner, style and behaviour of the courtesan, so she was clearly a significant element in society. And a severe distinction is made between the courtesan and the common prostitute.

The courtesans were elegant, resourceful, accomplished women of many talents and of a high degree of education. Many were as skilled as men in the arts of debate and intellectual conversation and they were a social asset. They had splendid houses, were welcomed at social gatherings and the older courtesans often taught the young sons and daughters of nobles in social arts, singing, dancing, and music. They enjoyed certain privileges and were considered models of correct behaviour.

Kama Sutra

Indian literature is full of episodes and stories which demonstrate the high respect accorded the courtesans, and it was not unknown for such a woman to form a permanent attachment with loyalty and dignity. Although entirely dependent upon men for their living and their status, the courtesans enjoyed a much freer life than the wives. It is they who would go on the picnics, on the midnight bathing trips; who would converse and discuss with the men – while the devoted (but happy) wife would remain watchful in the shadows.

This brief background reveals the particular place that sex and sexual activity held in early Hindu society. The important thing to remember is that its practise was considered an art – something that repaid study and work. This is, of course, quite different from the attitude to sex which prevails even today. The sex for pleasure principle is probably firmly established, but there is still a strong reaction to the idea that it should be specially studied. A young man, today, who took up, for example, photography would be expected to spend money, time and energy pursuing his hobby. Were he to be seen putting a similar weight of investment into sex he would be seen as rather suspect.

Not so the *nagarika*. He spent time and energy on his business dealings; he learned how to train his fighting animals and his talking birds; he spent time on hydraulics and mineralogy – and he spent just as much time studying *Kama*. In this way sex became an integral part of life – an art, a pleasure, a sacrament. As noted earlier, his society was strictly regulated, the people he could and could not contemplate having sexual relations with were clearly defined: it was never a sexual free-for-all.

The Secrets of Sex

The section of the *Kama Sutra* which deals with sexual instruction opens with a short chapter which gets down to the essentials with no preliminaries. In this case the essential are: genital size (male and female), degree of passion (or sexual excitement) and the time taken for both to reach orgasm.

But first, a note on language. One aspect of writing and talking

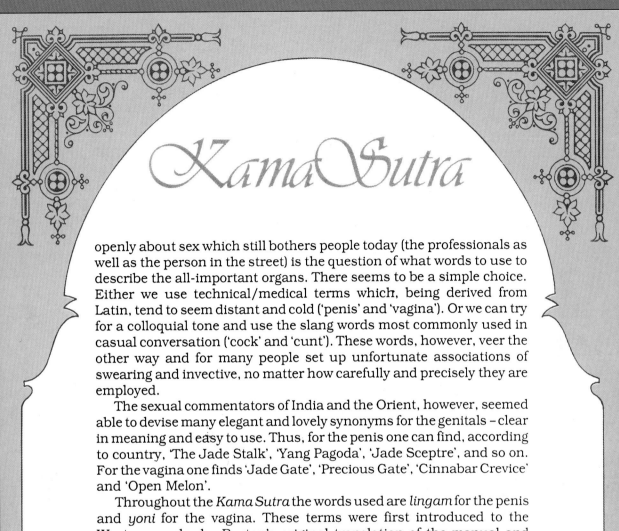

Kama Sutra

openly about sex which still bothers people today (the professionals as well as the person in the street) is the question of what words to use to describe the all-important organs. There seems to be a simple choice. Either we use technical/medical terms which, being derived from Latin, tend to seem distant and cold ('penis' and 'vagina'). Or we can try for a colloquial tone and use the slang words most commonly used in casual conversation ('cock' and 'cunt'). These words, however, veer the other way and for many people set up unfortunate associations of swearing and invective, no matter how carefully and precisely they are employed.

The sexual commentators of India and the Orient, however, seemed able to devise many elegant and lovely synonyms for the genitals – clear in meaning and easy to use. Thus, for the penis one can find, according to country, 'The Jade Stalk', 'Yang Pagoda', 'Jade Sceptre', and so on. For the vagina one finds 'Jade Gate', 'Precious Gate', 'Cinnabar Crevice' and 'Open Melon'.

Throughout the *Kama Sutra* the words used are *lingam* for the penis and *yoni* for the vagina. These terms were first introduced to the Western reader by Burton's original translation of the manual and became widely used (not just in an Indian context), and they are, at some level, familiar to most people. So these, therefore, are the words that will be used throughout this commentary.

The opening of Vatsyayana's section on sex (*Kinds of Union*) seems didactic; he appears to be making a definite, incontrovertible statement. There are, he asserts, three classes of man, which he calls the hare, the bull and the horse according to the size of their lingam. Similarly, there are three classes of woman, defined according to the depth of her yoni, and these he calls the female deer, the mare and the female elephant.

No measurements are given, but a later sex manual called the *Ananga Ranga*, which draws on the *Kama Sutra* and other books for its information, does suggest that the lingam of the hare is about five inches long, that of the bull is seven inches and that of the horse up to ten inches. The depth of the deer's yoni is about five inches, that of the mare about seven inches and that of the elephant around ten inches. Physical characteristics are deduced from these dimensions, too, so

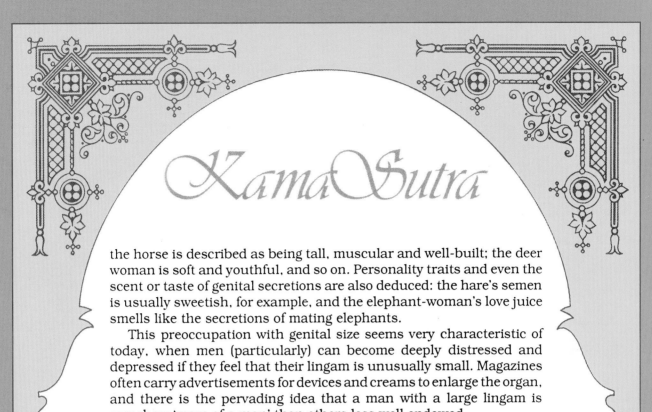

Kama Sutra

the horse is described as being tall, muscular and well-built; the deer woman is soft and youthful, and so on. Personality traits and even the scent or taste of genital secretions are also deduced: the hare's semen is usually sweetish, for example, and the elephant-woman's love juice smells like the secretions of mating elephants.

This preoccupation with genital size seems very characteristic of today, when men (particularly) can become deeply distressed and depressed if they feel that their lingam is unusually small. Magazines often carry advertisements for devices and creams to enlarge the organ, and there is the pervading idea that a man with a large lingam is somehow 'more of a man' than others less well endowed.

To the modern reader this section of the *Kama Sutra* might seem naive or even ignorant. Sex research over the last twenty or more years has proved conclusively that the average size of the erect lingam is about six inches. We also know there is no direct correlation between physical appearance and genital size – a slim, delicate man may possess a very large lingam, just as a massively built man may possess one slimmer and slighter. We also know that the taste of semen and genital secretions can change according to diet. So at first glance this opening salvo could seem likely to create anxiety. But that is only if it is interpreted through our modern minds.

For Vatsyayana goes on to enumerate the variations of sexual union possible between the six types of lingam and yoni and defines nine altogether. He states, quite rightly, that the 'equal' unions are the most successful – that is hare/deer, bull/mare and horse/elephant. He then divides the six 'mismatches' into sub categories, listing 'high' unions and 'low' unions. High unions are when the male exceeds the female in size: low unions are when the woman exceeds the man in size.

Putting a value judgement on the mismatches, the writer believes that high unions are preferable to low unions because with the latter it is difficult to satisfy the female.

Two things are happening in this preliminary exposition. First, the author is saying that genitals come in various sizes and that none of them is better or worse than any other. The idea that a deer-man might feel inferior to the horse-man never occurs: what you yourself have is adequate and perfect for the battle of love. This is in complete contrast

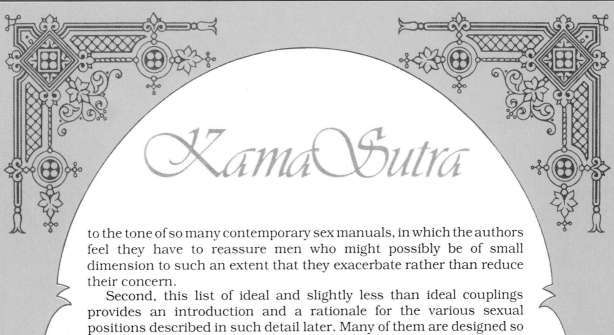

KamaSutra

to the tone of so many contemporary sex manuals, in which the authors feel they have to reassure men who might possibly be of small dimension to such an extent that they exacerbate rather than reduce their concern.

Second, this list of ideal and slightly less than ideal couplings provides an introduction and a rationale for the various sexual positions described in such detail later. Many of them are designed so that both partners can get the maximum pleasure out of their union. As we shall see, he shows how certain ways of lying down, certain kinds of thrust, can stretch a small yoni or tighten a particularly large one.

We know, today, that the vagina is extremely elastic and, with appropriate preparation and foreplay, can easily accommodate a large penis. We also know that in long-standing, monogamous relationships a couple's sex organs adjust to match each other perfectly, and techniques for stretching the one or enlarging the other are simply not required.

However, as we have seen in the previous chapter, the people for whom the *Kama Sutra* was a major text book did not lead lives of sexual monogamy. Not only might a *nagarika* have several wives, he would also enjoy the favours of courtesans now and then. So in the course of a year his lingam might well meet yonis of many sizes and many experiences. The *Kama Sutra* reminds him to be aware of this and shows him how to prepare for it.

After this statement there comes a very brief note, or reminder, that individuals have varying sex drives, and these are categorized (for men and women) as small, middling and intense. The man of small passion, it is said, doesn't fancy sexual union much, his semen is scanty and he dislikes being warmly embraced by a woman. There is an implication here that a person's sex-drive remains constant throughout his or her sexually active life, which is not necessarily true, but the author is probably merely reminding his readers that sex life is full of variety and that everyone is different. Later on in the *Kama Sutra* there are suggestions concerning sex aids and aphrodisiacs which might stimulate those of small passions to rather more intense ones.

One of the charming aspects of the way in which the *Kama Sutra* is written is that every so often its author sets up a proposition and then

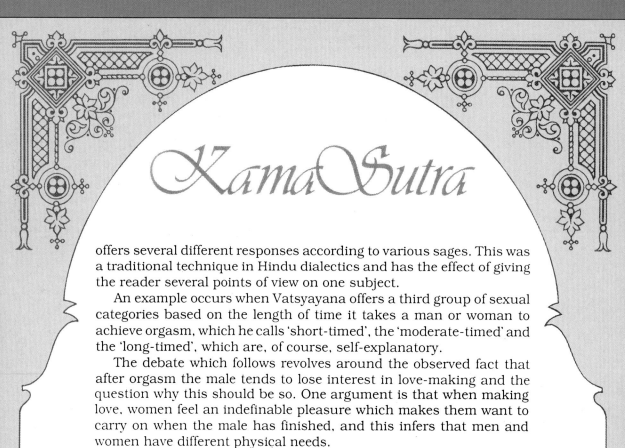

Kama Sutra

offers several different responses according to various sages. This was a traditional technique in Hindu dialectics and has the effect of giving the reader several points of view on one subject.

An example occurs when Vatsyayana offers a third group of sexual categories based on the length of time it takes a man or woman to achieve orgasm, which he calls 'short-timed', the 'moderate-timed' and the 'long-timed', which are, of course, self-explanatory.

The debate which follows revolves around the observed fact that after orgasm the male tends to lose interest in love-making and the question why this should be so. One argument is that when making love, women feel an indefinable pleasure which makes them want to carry on when the male has finished, and this infers that men and women have different physical needs.

This view is countered with the argument that when this happens it is because a short-time man is making love with a long-time woman and she is upset because he has finished before her, and if she is enjoying the sensations of being aroused and drawn to her climax then naturally she will wish to continue loveplay.

Then there is the argument that the woman takes some time to become aroused and, at the beginning of intercourse, finds the thrusts of a lover difficult to cope with. However, as her passion increases she gets more and more excited and only after her orgasm does she wish to stop.

Linked in with this is the concept of female ejaculation. The *Kama Sutra* refers to female emission as 'the fall of semen' and seems to equate this phenomenon exactly with male ejaculation – as the manifestation of orgasm (a word, incidentally, not used in the book). So some of the arguments are based on the idea that women ejaculate throughout intercourse, whereas men only ejaculate at their climax; others depend on the idea that women and men ejaculate in the same way and at the same time in their individual sexual cycles.

Until comparatively recently it was assumed that the early sexologists simply confused the natural vaginal lubrications of the aroused female with something equivalent to the male's emission or ejaculation, and knowing that women do not produce 'semen', the whole passage would be seen as fanciful and mistaken. However, fairly intense and

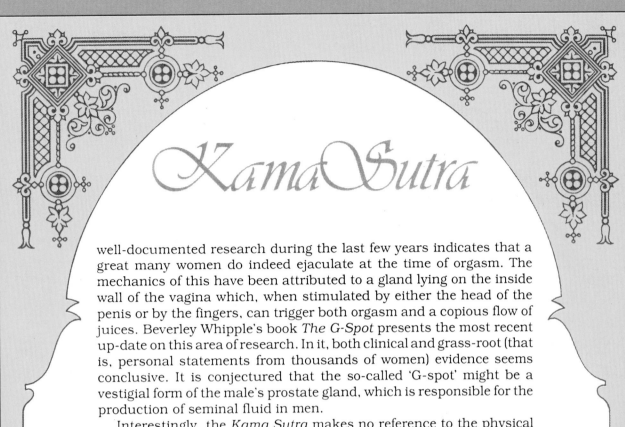

well-documented research during the last few years indicates that a great many women do indeed ejaculate at the time of orgasm. The mechanics of this have been attributed to a gland lying on the inside wall of the vagina which, when stimulated by either the head of the penis or by the fingers, can trigger both orgasm and a copious flow of juices. Beverley Whipple's book *The G-Spot* presents the most recent up-date on this area of research. In it, both clinical and grass-root (that is, personal statements from thousands of women) evidence seems conclusive. It is conjectured that the so-called 'G-spot' might be a vestigial form of the male's prostate gland, which is responsible for the production of seminal fluid in men.

Interestingly, the *Kama Sutra* makes no reference to the physical details of the female genital organs; the inner and outer lips are not mentioned, nor is the clitoris (not even by inference), nor is anything that could be interpreted as the G-spot. But this may well have been because the study of anatomy had not caught up with the direct observations made by people making love. But, as we know, it often takes science and research quite some time to produce 'authentic' evidence of something ordinary people have experienced or known intuitively for a long time. The sages who were happy to debate the nature of the female orgasm at length quite simply knew that women did enjoy emissions of fluid and these were more intense and more copious at the moments of greatest excitement. We can supply the medical textbooks; but they were more concerned about what was happening rather than about why and how it happened.

The argument continues with the puzzling question as to whether men and women feel and react in the same way, or whether there are crucial differences. One theme is that since a couple when making love 'have different work to do' – that is the male is active, the female acted upon – then it follows they should react and sense things in equally different ways. That is answered by the notion that while men and women might have to take different roles, the object of the exercise is the same for both and there is no reason to imagine they experience different degrees of pleasure.

The conclusion is that men and women do indeed feel the same kind of sensations and pleasures when making love, but that, bearing in

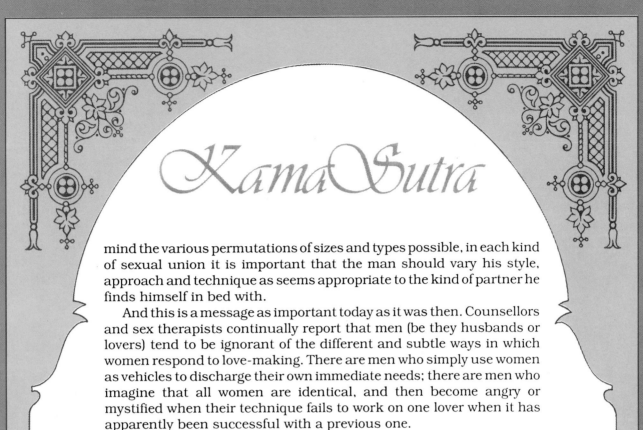

Kama Sutra

mind the various permutations of sizes and types possible, in each kind of sexual union it is important that the man should vary his style, approach and technique as seems appropriate to the kind of partner he finds himself in bed with.

And this is a message as important today as it was then. Counsellors and sex therapists continually report that men (be they husbands or lovers) tend to be ignorant of the different and subtle ways in which women respond to love-making. There are men who simply use women as vehicles to discharge their own immediate needs; there are men who imagine that all women are identical, and then become angry or mystified when their technique fails to work on one lover when it has apparently been successful with a previous one.

The message of the *Kama Sutra* is that there are an infinite number of variations between people and that any sexual incompatibility can be resolved by study, by art and by application of different techniques. Many of today's males would benefit from remembering this simple, human observation.

This section concludes with the reminder that when a man enjoys his first intercourse of the night then he is feeling extremely excited and will reach his orgasm and conclusion very quickly. However, his speed diminishes and his time increases with subsequent unions on the same occasion. Women operate differently. For her, the first act of intercourse means a low sex drive and a long time before she achieves her peak. But subsequent unions mean an increase in passion and a diminishing in time.

At this point in the *Kama Sutra* the author adds a note on what he defines as 'the four kinds of love'.

The first is love acquired by continual habit. This, he states, is love resulting from the constant and continual performance of some act. This seems to be a kind of addictive desire, that of wanting to repeat an experience which has been greatly enjoyed. The act of sexual intercourse is given as an example, but so are the love of hunting, drinking and gambling.

The next is love resulting from the imagination. This is a desire to experience activities to which one is not regularly accustomed. Oral sex is offered as an example. (Although the *Kama Sutra* does have a section

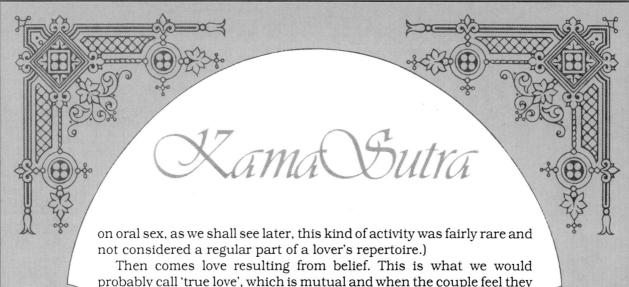

Kama Sutra

on oral sex, as we shall see later, this kind of activity was fairly rare and not considered a regular part of a lover's repertoire.)

Then comes love resulting from belief. This is what we would probably call 'true love', which is mutual and when the couple feel they really belong to one another.

Finally, love resulting from the perception of external objects, which indicates an acute awareness of the senses and of the world around, especially when the erotic lifestyle outlined earlier is followed.

After this general chapter, which the author considers quite adequate for intelligent and learned people, there follow more detailed instructions in the art of love.

The arts of love described fall into six sections: embracing, kissing, scratching with the nails, biting, striking and sexual positions. In each category different variations are described with precision and given particular names. This has led to the erroneous idea that the *Kama Sutra* is schematic, too technical and therefore heartless, and the idea grows that a couple might repair to their bed with an open copy in their hands saying, in effect, 'let's try the Congress of the Deer', which would, indeed, be mechanical and lacking in spontaneity and passion.

So it must be emphasised that all these gestures and positions were not intended, or prescribed, as individual practices but were, rather, expected to feature in the general and increasingly passionate flow of love-making. However, as already made clear, for the readers of the *Kama Sutra* sex and love-making were arts to be studied, so all the gestures and kinds of embraces and kisses had their own symbolic significance and examples of them can be found in painting, sculpture and poetry. We in the West tend to have lost this awareness of the symbolic gesture which carries a universal meaning wherever it is found. One of the few remaining examples is that of the Statue of Liberty in New York Harbour. The gesture of the woman holding aloft a flaming torch is powerful and instantly associated with freedom and the spirit of liberty. If that image, or a variation of it, appears on a poster, a label or even a T-shirt, then its significance and message is immediately understood.

Thus, in Indian art, if a temple carving shows a couple in one particular form of embrace the worshippers and visitors will immedi-

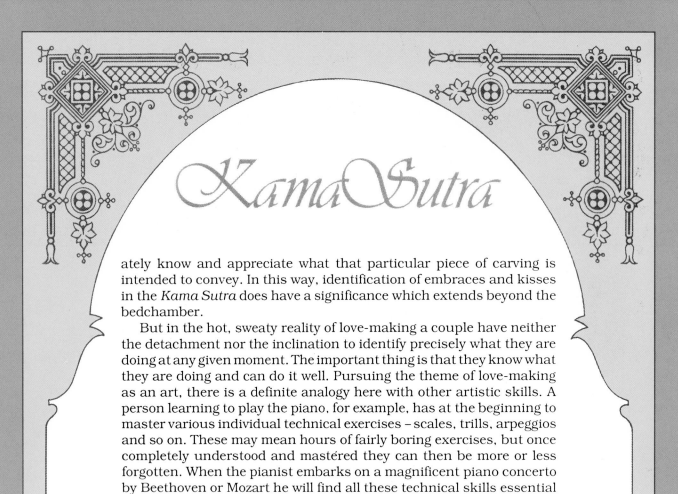

ately know and appreciate what that particular piece of carving is intended to convey. In this way, identification of embraces and kisses in the *Kama Sutra* does have a significance which extends beyond the bedchamber.

But in the hot, sweaty reality of love-making a couple have neither the detachment nor the inclination to identify precisely what they are doing at any given moment. The important thing is that they know what they are doing and can do it well. Pursuing the theme of love-making as an art, there is a definite analogy here with other artistic skills. A person learning to play the piano, for example, has at the beginning to master various individual technical exercises – scales, trills, arpeggios and so on. These may mean hours of fairly boring exercises, but once completely understood and mastered they can then be more or less forgotten. When the pianist embarks on a magnificent piano concerto by Beethoven or Mozart he will find all these technical skills essential and be able to use his technique naturally to enhance his interpretation.

So it is with love-making. A couple who have mastered the technical advice of the *Kama Sutra* can more or less forget it, but when embarking on a magnificent night of love will be able to bring their skills into play without a second thought and thus enhance their expressions of love and lust.

The *Kama Sutra*'s first detailed lesson concerns the embrace. In a sense all contact between the bodies of two lovers can be termed an embrace and the author emphasises that to him the embrace 'indicates the mutual love of a man and woman who have come together'. But even with this proviso in mind it is clear that an embrace has a wide range of implication, from a casual squeeze of affection to the deeply passionate entwining of limbs.

The first two kinds of embrace described take place only between people who are still getting to know each other and haven't yet quite made their intentions absolutely plain. So they may be regarded as the very first moves in the game of love, able to be taken on the level of flirtation but remaining open for further and more serious follow-up.

The 'touching embrace' is simply when a man makes an excuse to pass close to a woman and almost accidentally rubs his body against

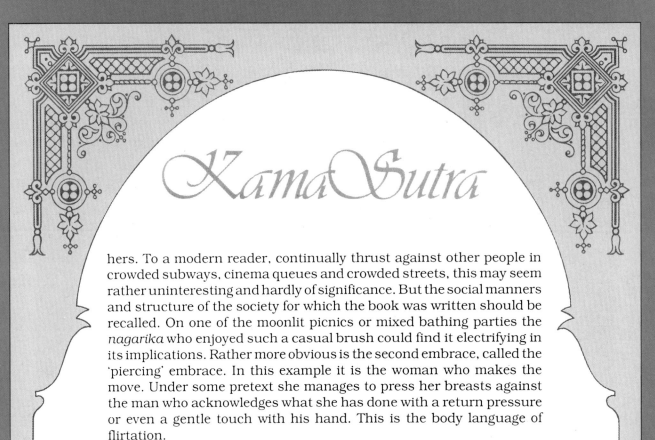

Kama Sutra

hers. To a modern reader, continually thrust against other people in crowded subways, cinema queues and crowded streets, this may seem rather uninteresting and hardly of significance. But the social manners and structure of the society for which the book was written should be recalled. On one of the moonlit picnics or mixed bathing parties the *nagarika* who enjoyed such a casual brush could find it electrifying in its implications. Rather more obvious is the second embrace, called the 'piercing' embrace. In this example it is the woman who makes the move. Under some pretext she manages to press her breasts against the man who acknowledges what she has done with a return pressure or even a gentle touch with his hand. This is the body language of flirtation.

Then, as the couple became more intimate and have made their mutual intentions clear, they can enjoy the 'rubbing embrace' which happens as their bodies rub closely against each other as they walk side by side. And when one presses the other's body forcibly up against a wall or pillar and leans on her or him, then this is called a 'pressing' embrace. All these four kinds of contact would be acceptable in public places and would perhaps cause a little amusement to the older people as they watched the young couple growing closer in this way.

The next two kinds of embrace belong to lovers who are intimate with each other, and are done in a standing position. In fact, these are the embraces most erotically portrayed on the great carved temples of Konarak, where legs, arms and bodies are sculpted in graceful, balletic positions and the position of hands and faces simmer with restrained eroticism.

First there is 'The Twining of a Creeper', when the woman clings to the man like a beautiful, flowering plant growing around a sturdy tree. She places her hand on the back of his head and bends it down towards her for a kiss and looks lovingly up at him. The other standing embrace pursues the imagery of nature and is called 'The Climbing of a Tree' with the man cast again in the role of tree. She places one of her feet on his and raises her other leg level with his thigh. One of her arms encircles his neck and the other rests on his shoulders as though she were about to climb up him. During both embraces the woman is instructed to make little sounds of singing or cooing.

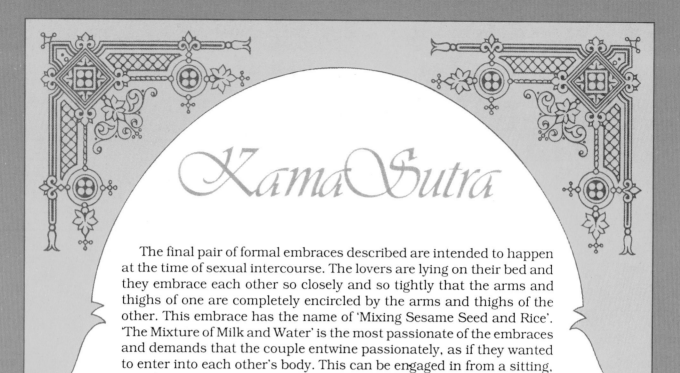

Kama Sutra

The final pair of formal embraces described are intended to happen at the time of sexual intercourse. The lovers are lying on their bed and they embrace each other so closely and so tightly that the arms and thighs of one are completely encircled by the arms and thighs of the other. This embrace has the name of 'Mixing Sesame Seed and Rice'. 'The Mixture of Milk and Water' is the most passionate of the embraces and demands that the couple entwine passionately, as if they wanted to enter into each other's body. This can be engaged in from a sitting, standing or lying position.

As a kind of footnote, four further embraces are noted, each referring to a particular part of the body. There is the 'Embrace of the Thighs', when one or both of the thighs of a lover are pressed forcibly between the partner's. There is the 'Embrace of the Mid-section' – that is, hips, loins and thighs. There is the 'Embrace of the Breasts', which involves the man asserting his naked chest against the bared breasts of his lover and pressing firmly. This is another embrace which can be enjoyed with one partner sitting on the other's knee. Then there is the particularly gentle and tender 'Embrace of the Forehead', when either lover touches the other's mouth, eyes and forehead with his or her own.

Vatsyayana notes that some people argue that 'shampooing' may be categorised as an embrace since it involves the touching of bodies. But he can't quite agree, because shampooing is 'performed at a different time, for a different purpose and has a different character'. The term 'shampooing' means in this context 'massage' and the oiling of bodies. From some later comments in the book it seems that then, as now, massage, while acceptable and important, might also have been used as a light excuse for certain intimacies which are not completely relevant to the concepts of love and regard symbolised by the list of embraces.

This short chapter ends on a note of refreshing realism. Actually, any embrace, even if it is not mentioned in the *Kama Sutra*, is admissible in the cause of sexual enjoyment if it helps to heighten passion. And while the couple are in the 'middle' stages of passion it is as well to follow the rules. But when excitement grows high and passion takes control then, in effect, anything goes.

Before discussing his next subject – kissing – Vatsyayana tries to

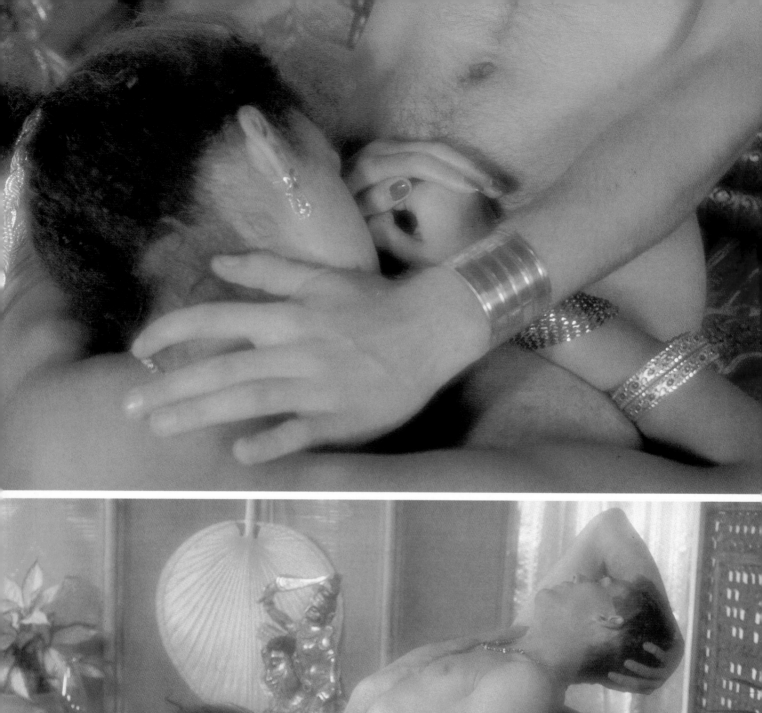

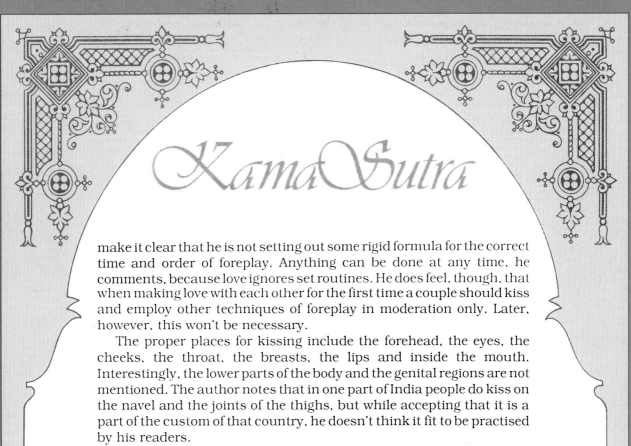

Kama Sutra

make it clear that he is not setting out some rigid formula for the correct time and order of foreplay. Anything can be done at any time, he comments, because love ignores set routines. He does feel, though, that when making love with each other for the first time a couple should kiss and employ other techniques of foreplay in moderation only. Later, however, this won't be necessary.

The proper places for kissing include the forehead, the eyes, the cheeks, the throat, the breasts, the lips and inside the mouth. Interestingly, the lower parts of the body and the genital regions are not mentioned. The author notes that in one part of India people do kiss on the navel and the joints of the thighs, but while accepting that it is a part of the custom of that country, he doesn't think it fit to be practised by his readers.

It is, however, the mouth which is of supreme importance, because the coming together of lips, the probing of the tongue and the exchange of body fluids involved in a kiss represent a close approximation to sexual intercourse itself.

Bearing this in mind, the teacher begins by explaining three kinds of kiss most suitable for a young girl. These kisses are gentle, exploratory and tender. The 'nominal' kiss is when the girl simply brushes the mouth of her lover with her own. When she is a little more confident she may wish to touch the man's lip when he presses it to her mouth. To this end she should move her lower lip only, not the upper one. This is the 'throbbing' kiss. Thirdly, she can just touch her lover's lip with her tongue while, at the same time, holding his hands.

Other kisses listed are not in any way 'advanced', but simply catalogued as it were according to the position of the faces and the amount of pressure used. Interesting is what is known as 'the greatly pressed kiss', which requires the lower lips to be held between two fingers, touched with the tongue and then pressed strongly. There is, too, the 'Kiss of the Upper Lip' in which the man kisses the woman's upper lip and she in turn kisses his lower lip. A 'Clasping Kiss' is when one partner takes both lips of the other between her or his lips. But a woman may only accept this kind of kiss from a man who has no facial hair. Kisses in which tongues mingle deeply, touching the inside of the mouth and the palate are called 'Fighting of the Tongue'. Listed too are

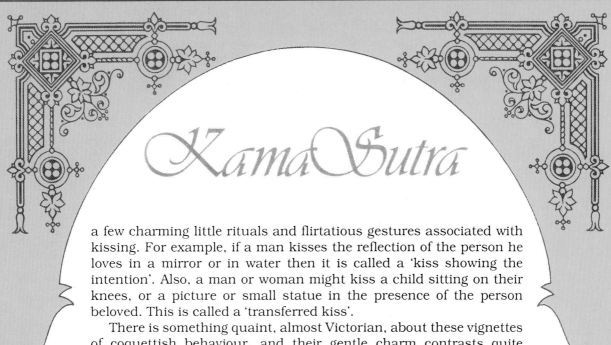

Kama Sutra

a few charming little rituals and flirtatious gestures associated with kissing. For example, if a man kisses the reflection of the person he loves in a mirror or in water then it is called a 'kiss showing the intention'. Also, a man or woman might kiss a child sitting on their knees, or a picture or small statue in the presence of the person beloved. This is called a 'transferred kiss'.

There is something quaint, almost Victorian, about these vignettes of coquettish behaviour, and their gentle charm contrasts quite strongly with the acceptance of unbridled passion and hectic love-making evidenced elsewhere in this erotic treatise. It is quite possible that the section on kissing was primarily aimed at young lovers, youths and girls just embarking on romance. As we have seen, the *Kama Sutra* takes a very moral and orthodox view of marriage itself and insists that – even though a marriage was ultimately arranged by the respective families – the young couple should have ample time to get to know each other and enjoy each other's company without restriction. Kisses would certainly represent the first step towards a more intimate relationship, though the girl would have to remain a virgin until marriage.

The next section of the *Kama Sutra* deals with a slightly more sophisticated element of love-making – scratching with the fingernails, biting with the teeth and striking with the hands or fists. So elaborated and detailed are the prescriptions for these particular evidences of passion that quite a few modern readers have come to see the book as some kind of sado-masochistic text and concluded that at the time the book was written lovers went out of their way to cause each other grievous bodily harm.

But, as always, we must try to get the text in proportion. The author is not saying that these things must be done or should be done. He is adopting his sensible, realistic approach and acknowledging that when passions are high and love-making reaches a peak, then expression of ecstatic feelings can take many forms. All the ancient books of love and sex instruction from the East include sections on scratching and biting and, indeed, the fingernails were an important cosmetic detail for sexually active people. The *Kama Sutra* suggests that people with a high sex-drive might have their fingernails cut with two or three points

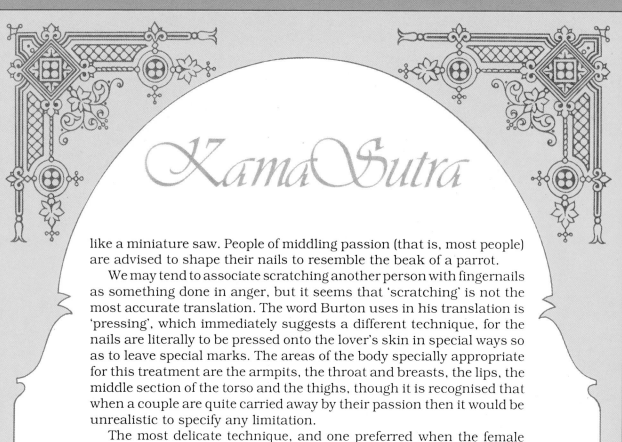

Kama Sutra

like a miniature saw. People of middling passion (that is, most people) are advised to shape their nails to resemble the beak of a parrot.

We may tend to associate scratching another person with fingernails as something done in anger, but it seems that 'scratching' is not the most accurate translation. The word Burton uses in his translation is 'pressing', which immediately suggests a different technique, for the nails are literally to be pressed onto the lover's skin in special ways so as to leave special marks. The areas of the body specially appropriate for this treatment are the armpits, the throat and breasts, the lips, the middle section of the torso and the thighs, though it is recognised that when a couple are quite carried away by their passion then it would be unrealistic to specify any limitation.

The most delicate technique, and one preferred when the female partner is just a young girl, is called 'sounding', which simply means pressing with the nails very softly and without leaving any mark. This light touch may send a frisson of unexpected delight through the body and cause the fine hairs on the arms to stand on end. A single curved mark left by a deeper pressure is called a 'half moon', and two half moons opposite each other are a 'circle'. There are several other marks specified, each with its own particular name. A curved mark made with all five nails, and left on the breast, is called the 'peacock's foot' and a note adds that a great deal of skill is required to be able to do it properly and that those who do it are, therefore, seeking notice and praise.

Part of the function of scratching and biting seems to have been to draw public notice to the fact that a love affair was going on. A young woman showing love bites or nail marks on her breast or throat was an object of admiration. And the reader is reminded that such marks should not be made on married women – though certain marks may be made on their private parts as souvenirs or reminders of love.

Love marks also acted as reminders for the participants, too. It was considered appropriate for a man to mark his wife or lover in this way when he was about to go on a journey, so that she would remember him in his absence. For a woman or man to see the marks of their lover on their body similarly acts as a constant reminder of the other person. If there are no marks then the love is likely to dwindle in much the same way as it would if the couple hadn't made love for some time.

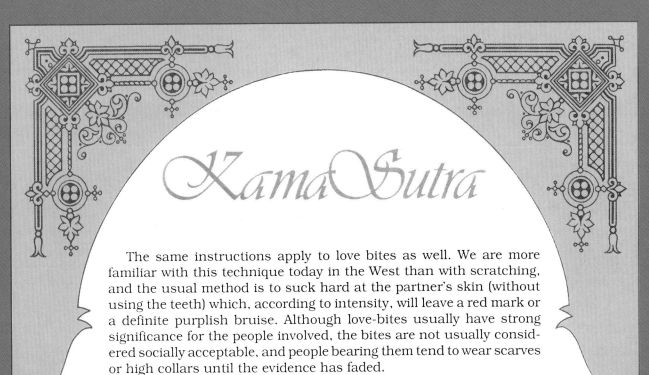

Kama Sutra

The same instructions apply to love bites as well. We are more familiar with this technique today in the West than with scratching, and the usual method is to suck hard at the partner's skin (without using the teeth) which, according to intensity, will leave a red mark or a definite purplish bruise. Although love-bites usually have strong significance for the people involved, the bites are not usually considered socially acceptable, and people bearing them tend to wear scarves or high collars until the evidence has faded.

Such reactions were, of course, unknown at the time the *Kama Sutra* was compiled and, as with scratch or nail marks, love bites were worn with pleasure and honour. Eight kinds of bite are listed, and for a lover to achieve his desired effect some skill would be needed. It is perhaps relevant to remember that painting elaborate designs on the skin was an important feature of Oriental cosmetics, especially for feast days and big social events. The very precise patterns made by teeth and nails would thus be seen as a particularly powerful form of personal adornment.

Among the bites, interestingly, is the 'biting of a boar', which consists of several broad rows of marks near to one another with red intervals. This is made on the breasts and shoulders and is particularly associated with highly passionate people. The 'hidden bite', which just leaves the skin red, is made specially on the lower lip and the 'string of points'. when small sections of skin are bitten with all the teeth, can be done on the throat, the armpit and the joints of the thighs.

The author notes that, regarding all the various elements of foreplay and loveplay he is talking about, those which increase passion in a lover should be done right away in order to get the erotic temperature rising, while those which are simply done for amusement or for variety should be left until later.

Finally, he suggests that when a man bites a woman then she should return the compliment twice as strongly, offering two bruises to his one and so forth. She is also invited to start a love quarrel and then conclude it by grabbing him by the hair, shutting her eyes and biting him in various places.

Sexual intercourse can be compared to a quarrel, remarks Vatsyayana at one point, because of the contrarieties of love and its tendency

Kama Sutra

to dispute. Also, high passion can inspire lovers to strike each other, literally. There are four kinds of blow – that with the back of the hand, that with the fingers a little contracted, that with the fist and that with the open palm of the hand. The special parts of the body for striking are the shoulders, the head, the space between the breasts, the back, the middle part of the body and the sides. There are also particular sounds associated with each kind of blow, a litany of noises expressing pain, praise, a request to stop, or a request for more; and it is suggested that noises like those made by birds (parrot, sparrow, flamingo etc.) could be used. And while the woman is being made love to, the space between her breasts should be struck with the back of the hand, slowly at first but faster as the excitement of intercourse increases.

Read in cold blood, these sections of the *Kama Sutra* give the impression that for the 2nd century Hindus love-making must have been a noisy, passionate and quite violent encounter. But virtually all the techniques enumerated are quite familiar to today's lovers – if not all at the same time. Most of us would probably find it hard to imitate the cry of the flamingo when gripped with passion, but people do make a wide variety of sounds when making love. Many people enjoy the idea of bites and blows of a mild nature; spanking is particularly popular. All this stops well short of sado-masochistic practices, of course, which tend to be an end in themselves, whereas the techniques suggested by the *Kama Sutra* are offered as just a part of the whole range of physical possibilities available to inventive lovers. 'The various modes of enjoyment are not for all times or all persons', says the text, 'but they should only be used at the proper time, and in the proper places'.

The Positions of Love

As we have seen, the *Kama Sutra* describes the caressing and stimulating actions and gestures which a loving couple might use in ritualistic detail. Distinction is made between techniques designed to turn a man or woman on, and those which can be used when passion is running high for variety or just for fun. And then, in the by now familiar footnote of reason, the author usually adds that it doesn't

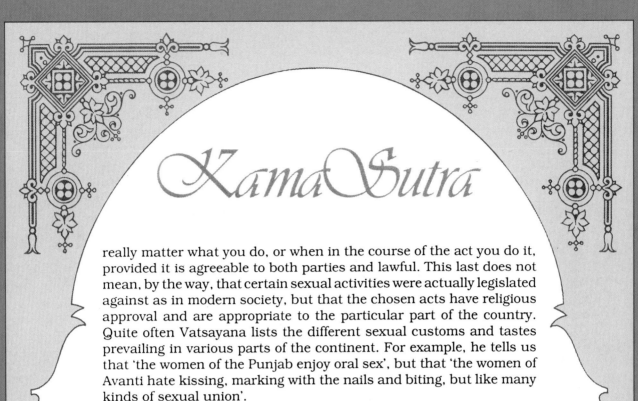

Kama Sutra

really matter what you do, or when in the course of the act you do it, provided it is agreeable to both parties and lawful. This last does not mean, by the way, that certain sexual activities were actually legislated against as in modern society, but that the chosen acts have religious approval and are appropriate to the particular part of the country. Quite often Vatsayana lists the different sexual customs and tastes prevailing in various parts of the continent. For example, he tells us that 'the women of the Punjab enjoy oral sex', but that 'the women of Avanti hate kissing, marking with the nails and biting, but like many kinds of sexual union'.

The section devoted to positions recommended for sexual union is, perhaps, the most celebrated passage in the *Kama Sutra*: to Western eyes many of them seem uncomfortable, too athletic to achieve, and difficult if not impossible. Yet at the same time they remain deeply exciting and suggest the possibilities of fluid, flexible, ecstatic and – above all – equal kinds of union. For centuries the West has, in practical terms, known only one basic position for coition, the famous 'missionary position', in which the woman lies passively on her back and the man works on top of her.

Alfred Kinsey, in *Sexual Behaviour in the Human Male* (1948) pointed out that this custom is involved in early and later Church history and reminds us that 'there was a time in the history of the Christian Church when the utilisation of any other except the present-day position was made a matter for confession'. Why – and how – the Church managed to impose this on the population seems mysterious; nevertheless, it was indeed so. It is interesting to note that most Western pornography, particularly of the 17th and 18th centuries, shows or describes almost every sexual act except the statutory one, another indication of pornography's subversive role.

By the time Richard Burton's first translation of the *Kama Sutra* appeared, the sex life of the average Western couple was boring, monotonous and routine. Women understood that sex was a necessary duty, first to produce children and second to satisfy the animal needs of their husbands. And their husbands' own ignorance of sexual variety and lack of knowledge of (or interest in) womens' needs meant that nothing came along to alter this view. A reading of the *Kama Sutra* at

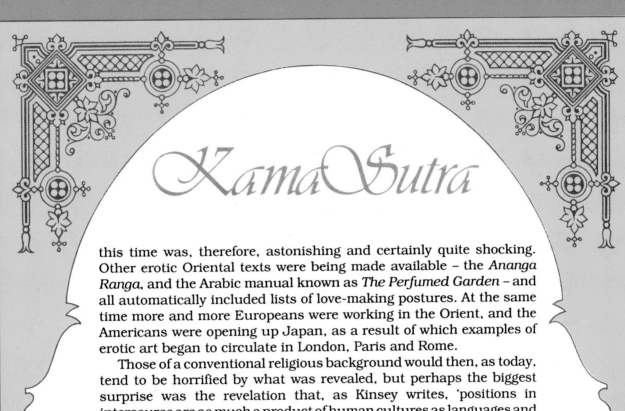

Kama Sutra

this time was, therefore, astonishing and certainly quite shocking. Other erotic Oriental texts were being made available – the *Ananga Ranga*, and the Arabic manual known as *The Perfumed Garden* – and all automatically included lists of love-making postures. At the same time more and more Europeans were working in the Orient, and the Americans were opening up Japan, as a result of which examples of erotic art began to circulate in London, Paris and Rome.

Those of a conventional religious background would then, as today, tend to be horrified by what was revealed, but perhaps the biggest surprise was the revelation that, as Kinsey writes, 'positions in intercourse are as much a product of human cultures as languages and clothing, and that the common English-American position is rare in some other cultures'.

Scholars believe that originally the *Kama Sutra*, the *Ananga Ranga* and other texts were decorated with illustrations of the various positions. Inevitably, after all these centuries, these no longer exist but there is a wealth of relevant Indian erotic art dating mainly from the 18th and 19th centuries. Many of these paintings represent quite clearly positions detailed in the *Kama Sutra*. This means we have a fairly good idea of what they looked like, and it also shows the *Kama Sutra's* influence down the ages as efficient in its way as the Church in imposing particularly acceptable sexual positions on a population.

Discussing 'various kinds of congress', Vatsyayana returns immediately to the point with which he started his discourse on the practicalities of sex: genital size. And the first three positions he offers concern the deer-woman (who has the smallest yoni). She may adopt 'the widely opened position', the 'yawning position' or 'the position of the wife of Indra'. All these positions are designed to help her widen her yoni to accommodate a larger than appropriate lingam. The male partner is urged to apply a lubricant to the yoni in order to make entry easier.

Widely Open Position: the woman lies back, lowers her head and raises her middle part towards the man, who may kneel or squat between her legs.

The Yawning Position: here she lies back, raises her thighs and keeps them wide apart throughout love-making.

Kama Sutra

Position of the Wife of Indra, or the 'Indrani' position: the woman lies back and draws her thighs up so that her knees are close against her flanks. This position, the book notes, is quite different and must be learned through practise. Certainly, to draw the thighs back and keep them pressed against the body in this way does demand a certain flexibility, though in practise pressure from the man's own body would help to maintain the position.

The next three positions described are particularly suitable for those occasions when the woman's yoni is too deep to match the size of the man's lingam.

The Clasping Position: the woman lies flat on her back, her arms stretched out beyond her head. The man lies directly on top of her, with all parts of his body from legs to hands touching hers as far as possible. If, as would mostly happen, the man is taller than the woman, then a cushion placed at her feet will support his feet at the appropriate height. This position can also be done with the couple lying on their sides, facing each other. The *Kama Sutra* states that the man should lie on his left side and the woman on her right – a rule to be observed when lying with all kinds of women.

The Pressing Position: this is an extension of the previous position. Once love-making has begun and the lingam has been inserted into the yoni, then the woman should bring her thighs together as tightly as possible, thus holding the lingam firmly in place.

The Mare's Position: as before, the woman brings her legs tightly together and forcibly holds the lingam in her yoni. The manual remarks that this is difficult and learned through practise and experience, but doesn't make it clear exactly how the lingam is 'forcibly' held – whether by hand or by the contraction of the vaginal muscles. During the last decades countless women have learned that by practising rhythmic contraction and relaxation of their vaginal muscles they have been able to strengthen the pelvic floor and tighten their vaginal muscles considerably. These are the well-known Kegel exercises. There is no instruction in the *Kama Sutra* that women might do anything remotely resembling this, but such exercises do feature in Yoga and Tantric practises, so it is quite possible that this was an automatic, natural ability.

Kama Sutra

The Rising Position: the female lies back and raises her thighs straight up. She can be sitting on her partner's thighs and he can assist by holding her thighs.

Yawning Position II: here she raises her legs and places them on her lover's shoulders.

Pressed Position: here she bends her knees, raises her legs and presses her feet against the chest of her lover. By clasping her round the thighs he can pull her very close towards him.

Half-pressed Position: one foot is pressed against the man's chest as in the previous position, but the other leg is allowed to stretch out around him.

Splitting Bamboo: so far, the positions listed have been fairly straight-forward and designed to make the best accommodation between lingams and yonis of various sizes. Now we move into a more elaborate area. For this position, the woman lies back, places one leg on her lover's shoulder and stretches the other leg right out. Then she reverses the procedure and changes the position of her legs alternately while congress is proceeding. The alternate stretching and bending of the legs would create exciting ripples and changes in the position and muscular tension of the yoni, and a change of position of the legs would need to coincide with each thrust of the lingam. Thus, each time the man thrusts inwards the woman would change the angles of her legs, and again as he withdraws. Obviously, this needs concentration and practise, the couple beginning fairly slowly to synchronise their movements but then, as they get used to it, moving faster and faster. It places great demands on the stamina and flexibility of the woman, but the ultimate effect must have been ecstatic. Young women of today who practise aerobics and yoga might find it stimulating to try – at least once!

Fixing a Nail: the woman lies back and places one of her legs so that the foot rests on the nape of her neck. The other leg is stretched out. Obviously, to achieve this a woman needs to be very flexible indeed and the *Kama Sutra* does state that this is 'learned by practise only'.

The Crab: when both the legs of the woman are contracted and the feet are fixed firmly on the region of her stomach.

The Packed Position: this is another position which is intended to

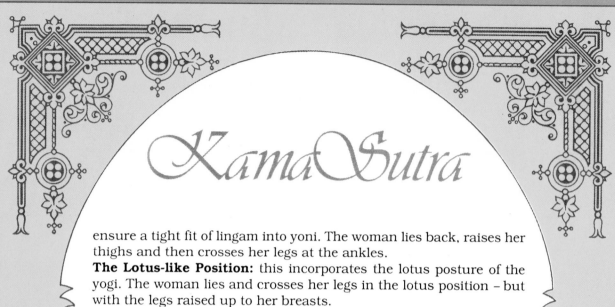

Kama Sutra

ensure a tight fit of lingam into yoni. The woman lies back, raises her thighs and then crosses her legs at the ankles.

The Lotus-like Position: this incorporates the lotus posture of the yogi. The woman lies and crosses her legs in the lotus position – but with the legs raised up to her breasts.

The Turning Position: the act of intercourse may start in any position provided the man can slowly turn around and, moving the woman as he does so, eventually enjoy her from behind without withdrawing his lingam from her yoni. Clearly this requires practise, but the willing co-operation of the woman it is not quite so arduous as it may sound.

All the positions described so far require the couple to be lying down or reclining in some way. The *Kama Sutra* now looks at the variety of positions available when the couple are standing up.

The Supported Position: this is the basic standing-up position practised both by intimate lovers in the privacy of their own homes and by whores in back alleys the world over. The couple can support each other with their own bodies or they can lean against a wall. Almost any comfortable variation of previously described positions may be used, from the basic face-to-face through to positions where one of the woman's legs is, perhaps, twined or hooked around the man's neck or shoulder.

Suspended Position: the man supports himself against a wall or pillar and clasps his hands together so that the woman can sit on them as on a swing. She then passes her arms around his neck and raises her thighs to his waist-level, resting her feet against the wall or pillar. When the couple are sure of their balance, she can move herself up and down on his lingam by pushing her feet against whatever the man is leaning upon.

These standing positions are vividly illustrated in the erotic temple sculptures already mentioned. There is an infinite grace about the figures; the movements seem fluid and effortless; hands and heads are turned and bent, positioned almost as if in a ballet, yet at the same time revealing true human tenderness and passion.

Animal Positions: a number of postures are named after the congress of particular animals – cows, goats, deer, horses, tigers and elephants etc. These names sometimes create difficulties for the modern Western

Kama Sutra

reader simply because modern, urban man's view of animals differs considerably from the views of the people for whom the *Kama Sutra* was written. Modern man tends to regard animals as inferior, dirty, dangerous and immoral. To call a woman a 'cow' is an insult, as it is to call her a 'dog'. To call a man a 'pig' or a 'goat' isn't intended to be flattering, either. To say that people are 'behaving like animals' means they are behaving very badly; the expression 'morals of the farmyard' indicates a complete loss of civilised behaviour, and so on.

A second's reflection will make one realise that these are valueless, purely emotional judgements. Animals, in fact, behave in a very civilised manner; their sexual behaviour is governed by seasonal impulse; their fighting is purely for territorial rights; even carnivores only kill for food. Rape, torture, murder, cruelty of all the kinds practised by man are unknown in the animal world. But, however rational one may try to be about this, the naming of sexual activities after kinds of animals strikes an uneasy chord in the West.

The ancient Hindu, on the other hand, lived much closer to the animal kingdom; he observed their coupling, their behaviour, their grace and beauty, and to him emulation of an animal meant the creation of a sympathetic bond through which he might absorb the particular powers of an animal – speed, strength, nobility and so on.

It must also be acknowledged that the various 'animal' postures are all variations of the rear-entry positions – not anal intercourse but, rather, approaching the yoni from behind. The woman might simply bend over, she might get down on all fours, she may lie on her face, but the congress of the cow, the deer, the goat and other animals all come down to variants of the same basic gesture. The *Kama Sutra* does urge couples to behave like their chosen animals when performing these positions through making appropriate noises, by scratching and biting. Although a *nagarika* and his ladies are town dwellers, towns at that time bore no resemblance to the extended urban centres of today. A town then might be no more than a collection of half a dozen houses. This means that nature, and the farmyard, were very close. The most urbanised people would hardly pass a day without seeing both domestic and wild animals about them. These positions all ensure the maximum exposure of the yoni and ease of its access to the male. This

Kama Sutra

implies full co-operation from the female partner, extending, as we have seen, into considerable physical effort. Nowhere is there any sense of the woman just lying back, closing her eyes and waiting for something to be done to her. The erotic illustrations only rarely show intercourse with the woman lying inertly on her back; they were always performed in sitting, squatting or half-reclining positions. The *Kama Sutra* suggests that it is a good idea to practise the more arduous positions first in water, since the buoyancy and support are a great help when trying new body postures.

But despite the demands made on the female partner, it remains clear that the man was required to use rather more sheer physical energy in love-making. Most of the time he is not merely doing the thrusting but also helping to support his partner by holding her waist, thighs or back in the chosen position. And the *Kama Sutra* realises that a man may occasionally get a little tired, especially if intercourse has been going on for some time and he hasn't yet reached a climax.

The 'work of a man' as it is called, remains as effective a model for efficient lovemaking today as it was when it was compiled. When she is lying on the bed he should distract her attention with interesting conversation and, as if by accident, almost unthinkingly, he should begin to loosen her clothes. If she decides to protest then he must overwhelm her with kisses. When he has an erection he must then caress her all over and pay special attention to various part of her body. She will certainly make signs and sounds of gentle protest, but he will override these with his kisses and the dexterity of his foreplay.

If she is a virgin he is advised first to get his hands on her breasts, which she will probably try to keep covered. He must do this gently but persuasively. Such a young girl will also probably keep her thighs pressed closely together and, again, it is the business of the man to place his hands between her thighs and slowly work them apart. Then he should stroke her hair and take her face between his hands, drawing it to him for kisses.

If his partner is a seasoned woman, says the text briskly, then they can do whatever it is that pleases them most. But whoever the woman is, the man is urged to take his cue from her, to touch those parts of her body 'on which she turns her eyes' and to realise from her gestures

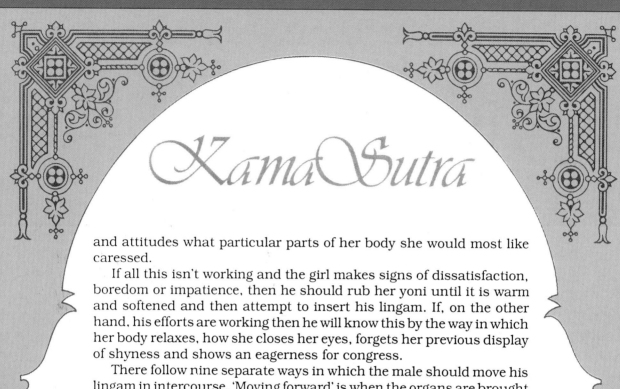

Kama Sutra

and attitudes what particular parts of her body she would most like caressed.

If all this isn't working and the girl makes signs of dissatisfaction, boredom or impatience, then he should rub her yoni until it is warm and softened and then attempt to insert his lingam. If, on the other hand, his efforts are working then he will know this by the way in which her body relaxes, how she closes her eyes, forgets her previous display of shyness and shows an eagerness for congress.

There follow nine separate ways in which the male should move his lingam in intercourse. 'Moving forward' is when the organs are brought together directly and he slides straight in. 'Churning' is when he holds his lingam in his hand and turns it in the yoni. 'Piercing' is when the yoni is lowered and the upper part is struck with the lingam. 'Rubbing' is the same but done to the lower part of the yoni. 'Pressing' is when the lingam is inserted deeply into the yoni and pressed firmly inside. When the lingam is removed a little way out of the yoni and then thrust back firmly to strike it, it is called 'giving a blow'. When only one part of the yoni is rubbed by the lingam it is called the 'Blow of a Boar', and the 'Blow of a Bull' involves rubbing both sides of the yoni in much the same way. The 'Sporting of a Sparrow' happens when the lingam is right inside the yoni and is moved up and down quickly but without being removed at all. This is recommended for the last phases of intercourse and this action does, of course, promote the man's orgasm fairly quickly.

If a woman perceives that her lover is getting a little tired, it is suggested that she should take over the 'work of a man' for a while. She must first ask his permission, and then lay him on his back and proceed to act his part, using as many of the gestures and techniques outlined above as are suitable for her. She can do this from scratch, as it were, or arrange for their positions to be reversed while intercourse is happening, but without allowing the lingam to slip out of her yoni. Once on top she can shake her hair loose, smile, breathe passionately and get down to work. Positions available to her are:

The Pair of Tongs: she squats or sits on top of him, drawing him into her, and holds his lingam inside by the pressure of her thighs for a long time.

Kama Sutra

The Spinning Top: this is possibly the most famous of all the *Kama Sutra* positions and involves the woman turning herself round on top of the man while keeping his lingam firmly inside her. This probably needs full participation from the male and is best attempted with him lying or half-reclining on the floor. But the man can raise the central part of his body up in a kind of arch, resting on his hands and feet. The woman is then poised above him to begin her spins. This act obviously demands considerable powers of technique, control and balance.

The Swing: this is a slightly more accessible version of the Spinning Top. Again the male raises his body in an arc and the woman impales herself on his erect lingam – but turned around so that her back is facing him. She then rocks back and forward, maintaining her balance by keeping her feet in contact with the ground.

There was a simple ritual for the moment when the woman in her turn becomes tired. She leans forward and places her forehead against that of her lover and, without releasing his lingam, ceases her movements. After a short space the man gently turns her over to begin the congress again with him in the superior position.

The *Kama Sutra* makes full allowance for sexual activity involving one man and several women or several men and one woman. Large, mixed orgies are not catered for. When a man enjoys two women at the same time it is called the 'united congress' and it is assumed that both women are equally in love with him. When a man enjoys many women at the same time this is called 'the congress of a herd of cows'. This is illustrated in several erotic prints. Usually the man is shown naked lying on his back, his arms and legs stretched wide. One woman squats on his erect lingam which is buried inside her. The man's hands and feet are all toying with the yonis of four women who stand by. The women would be expected to change places one by one.

When it is several men with one woman, they are each instructed to caress a part of her body in the appropriate way (mouth, breasts, loins) while one enjoys her. They then alternate their various roles.

People in the south of India have a congress in the anus, comments the author, and it is called 'the lower congress'. Since he pursues this information no further one must assume he added it for the sake of completeness only and does not recommend or approve it.

Kama Sutra

The chapter on oral sex is probably the most ambiguous section of the *Kama Sutra*. It is firmly related to the male; to the sucking of the lingam, and a strong sense of disapproval emanates from the pages. On the other hand the various techniques are described in great detail and much information is given.

In the sections on foreplay, intercourse and love-making techniques generally, oral-genital contact is simply not mentioned, either specifically or casually. This is because it was not seen as a part of regular, straightforward love-making but rather as a specialist function of the art of massage.

In fact, Vatsyayana associates the activity firmly with eunuchs. There are two kinds of eunuch he says – those who dress as women and conduct their lives in this guise and sometimes lead the life of a courtesan. Any acts which man might do on the loins of a woman are done in the mouths of these eunuchs.

The other kind of eunuch keeps his condition a secret and pursues the career of a masseur, which gives him plenty of opportunity to practise oral sex with his clients if he wishes to. It is noted, too, that male servants carry on mouth congress with their masters and that it is also practised between citizens (*nagarikas*) who know each other well. The women who would do it are all low class: the unchaste, the wanton, female servants and attendants, women who are not married to anyone but live by giving massage. The women in harems, when they are feeling sexually roused, will practise oral sex on each other's yonis and there are some men who do it to women.

There is in all this no suggestion of homosexuality in the sense that we understand that term today. In fact it is a fairly recent concept and would probably be incomprehensible to anyone living before the 19th century. At the time written about it seems that, generally speaking, sex was given three main functions: the production of children, the expression of passion and deep, abiding love, and an activity which gave fun and pleasure. In this last category almost anything was permissible (within the limits of spiritual guidance and local custom), so if a man wanted to enjoy oral sex with his servant or with his best friends it would be seen (if known about at all) as part of his natural and admirable search for different kinds of pleasure.

Kama Sutra

The sequence for the oral caress of the lingam begins with the shaft being held in the hand and the tip gently brushed between the lips. The sides may then be pressed with the lips and the teeth used, but delicately. The lingam is again inserted into the mouth and kissed as if it were the lower lips of a lover; it is then licked all over (including the tip) by the tongue, then put halfway into the mouth and forcefully kissed and sucked. Finally it is drawn completely into the mouth, pressed in to the end as far as it will go and sucked as if being swallowed. This last action is certainly what we have learned to call 'deep throat'.

Instructions for kissing the yoni are almost brutally brief. 'The way of doing this should be known from kissing the mouth'. One particular position is mentioned – 'the congress of the crow', which is what we would call 69, with the couple inverted so each may caress the other's genitals with their mouths. This can be performed lying or standing.

Mouth congress, says the *Kama Sutra* severely, should never be done by a learned Brahmin, by a minister of state or by a man of good reputation. it is, he admits, allowed by the general doctrines of *Kama* but argues that there is no reason why it should be practised. As an analogy he points out that there is plenty of evidence to prove that the flesh of dogs is edible, but that's no reason for wise men to start eating dog flesh. However, he concludes with the remark that since such acts are done in privacy and that man likes to try lots of different thing anyway, who knows what any person will do at any particular time or for any particular reason.

This ends the section of the *Kama Sutra* which is devoted exclusively to sexual activity and techniques. It is all-embracing and covers almost every aspect of the subject, making it as relevant today as it was when first written. Its relevance is more to do with attitude and spirit rather than to do with specific practices. We know much more about the way our bodies work today and have a much deeper insight into the ways in which desire can affect a person. But we also live in a much more complicated and tense society, so one of the messages of the book is to relax, take time to enjoy ourselves and each other and, above all, to seek knowledge about sex and treat it as a skill worth knowing about.

When studying the various positions listed in the *Kama Sutra* it is

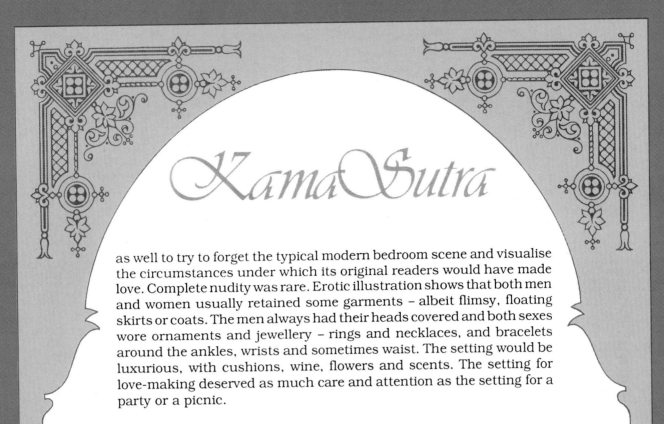

Kama Sutra

as well to try to forget the typical modern bedroom scene and visualise the circumstances under which its original readers would have made love. Complete nudity was rare. Erotic illustration shows that both men and women usually retained some garments – albeit flimsy, floating skirts or coats. The men always had their heads covered and both sexes wore ornaments and jewellery – rings and necklaces, and bracelets around the ankles, wrists and sometimes waist. The setting would be luxurious, with cushions, wine, flowers and scents. The setting for love-making deserved as much care and attention as the setting for a party or a picnic.

Little Extras

Set in the context of the living culture from which it sprang, the *Kama Sutra* offers a picture of a society which is at once highly organised and almost ritualistically ordered, and yet at the same time seems to offer what to modern eyes is a liberated and laid-back view of sex and sexual activity. Sexual perceptions were not, apparently, fetishistic in the way so many of those frequent in the West today are. For example, it has been noted that when making love couples usually retained some clothes and personal ornaments, and it is easy to imagine that these were the equivalent of the suspender belts, leather boots and spike-heeled shoes favored in so much erotic photography today.

But this is not so. For better or worse, these contemporary decorations are intended to concentrate interest on specific parts of the body (breasts, legs, buttocks) in a fetishistic way. The ornaments worn by the ancient Hindus were simply to make themselves attractive in the eyes of each other in a much more general way. In fact, it was one of society's rules that a wife must always appear beautifully dressed before her husband. A slovenly appearance, a casual appearance and total nudity were not countenanced. We have also noted that in the body of the *Kama Sutra*'s text there are no remarks about individual erogenous zones in either sex: no mention of the nipples, the clitoris, the foreskin, the scrotum, the perineum or the buttocks as good spots for stimulation.

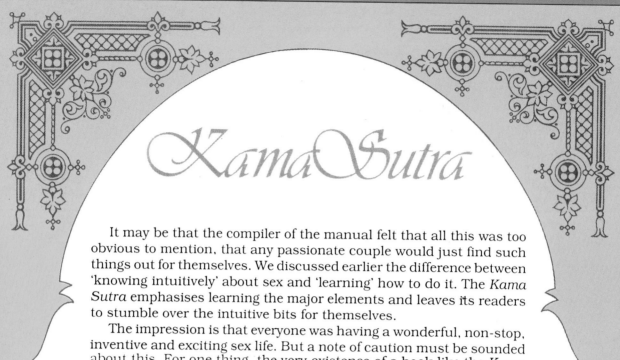

Kama Sutra

It may be that the compiler of the manual felt that all this was too obvious to mention, that any passionate couple would just find such things out for themselves. We discussed earlier the difference between 'knowing intuitively' about sex and 'learning' how to do it. The *Kama Sutra* emphasises learning the major elements and leaves its readers to stumble over the intuitive bits for themselves.

The impression is that everyone was having a wonderful, non-stop, inventive and exciting sex life. But a note of caution must be sounded about this. For one thing, the very existence of a book like the *Kama Sutra*, not to mention all the other sex manuals of India, Arabia and Japan, suggests that people needed to know; that left to their own devices and desires they might well make foolish mistakes and suffer the same sort of sexual problems that are so rife today. Whether they were any more widely read and acted upon than the dozens of sex manuals written in this century are, we cannot really know. But, since the life of the senses (which included sexual response) was one of the three basic elements on which Hindu philosophy was built, we can perhaps assume that the books were at least read.

That the *Kama Sutra* includes passages on what we would call sex aids, and contains lists of recipes for aphrodisiacs and other sensation-enhancing potions, indicates that sexual problems were not actually unknown. One which was clearly important to the author, and therefore presumably to his readers, relates to the problem of the man who has a small lingam. As we have already emphasised, the *Kama Sutra* nowhere suggests that there is such a thing as a 'small lingam' or that such a thing is undesirable or a matter for major concern. The book simply takes the view that there are some lingams which are too small for the particular yoni they wish to enter.

In the same way it points out that there are some lingams which are too big for the yonis they wish to enter. It is a subtle distinction but has the effect of making no male feel inferior or superior about his physical endowments. Many of the positions for intercourse are designed to accommodate these differences, but the book admits that there are occasions when a little more is needed.

Always the first piece of advice to a man who is trying to make love to an 'elephant woman' – a woman with a large yoni – is to try and

stimulate her manually until she becomes excited, so that when it comes to congress any difference in dimension will be forgotten in the general excitement. But he can also make use of devices which are fitted to the lingam to increase its length or girth and thus make it completely fill a large yoni.

These prosthetics were called *Apadravyas* and should be made from materials such as gold, silver, copper, tin, ivory, wood or buffalo horn. They should be soft, cool and fit well, and ideally a man should have his own custom-built. There were simple rings with the external surface made rough – the equivalent of the modern textured condom which is designed to stimulate the woman. Any number of these rings could be worn at the same time, extending along the length of the lingam. While this would certainly increase the girth satisfactorily, such a device would also clearly be useful if a man was suffering from impotence.

In cases of emergency, when no previous provision has been made for such a need, then natural plants may be used, such as cucumbers and reeds made soft with oils and plant extracts. In this connection it is also noted, in a short chapter on the women of the royal harem, that they would use what we know as dildoes on each other at times when they needed to have their desires satisfied.

This situation would arise because there was only one man available to make love to several women and many of them were never received in the royal bed. Vatsyayana tells us that when the women of the harem felt sexy they would make their attendants or some of their female friends dress up as men and make love to them. For penetration they used bulbs, roots and fruits which were phallus shaped. Or they might lower themselves on the statue of a male figure which sported a large, erect lingam.

In southern India at this time it was a common practice for men to pierce the head of their lingams and insert various kinds of prosthetic into the hole made. The instructions for self-piercing are not for the squeamish and not to be imitated. Body piercing is quite popular at the moment and any part of the body can be pierced: nipples, clitoris, vaginal lips, foreskin and the glans of the penis itself. But to avoid infection and serious damage it should always be done by a professional who uses the correct, hygienic equipment and anaesthetics.

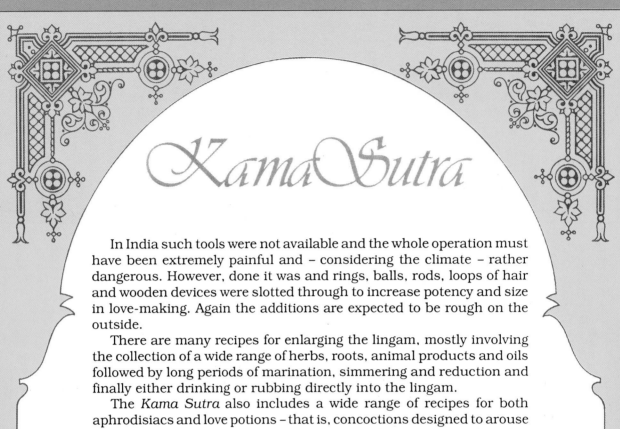

Kama Sutra

In India such tools were not available and the whole operation must have been extremely painful and – considering the climate – rather dangerous. However, done it was and rings, balls, rods, loops of hair and wooden devices were slotted through to increase potency and size in love-making. Again the additions are expected to be rough on the outside.

There are many recipes for enlarging the lingam, mostly involving the collection of a wide range of herbs, roots, animal products and oils followed by long periods of marination, simmering and reduction and finally either drinking or rubbing directly into the lingam.

The *Kama Sutra* also includes a wide range of recipes for both aphrodisiacs and love potions – that is, concoctions designed to arouse sexual passion in oneself and concoctions designed to make other people find one desirable. A typical potion described is milk mixed with sugar and having the testicle of a ram or goat boiled in it. A mixture of rice with sparrow eggs, boiled in milk with the addition of honey and ghee (clarified butter) gives permanent potency and enables a man to enjoy innumerable women.

Whether these potions literally worked is obviously doubtful, but the correct creation of aphrodisiacs and love potions was a specialised branch of Indian medicine and had religious approval. It is possible that the ointments and unguents which were rubbed into the lingam would create an immediate and temporary effect and if the user was psychologically conditioned to believe they would work then a placebo effect might result.

The *Kama Sutra* warns that no aphrodisiac should be used which is doubtful in effect, which is likely to cause injury to the genitals, which involves deliberately killing animals and that involves the use of impure things. Users are advised to go to the experts for information and prescriptions – scientists, magicians and older, trusted relatives.

This section of recipes brings the book to an end, and the author makes it clear that the use of such things is something of a last resort. He would prefer that women and men gained the object of their desire through good looks, personality, knowledge and charm. And he would prefer that lovers were retained through an efficient but loving sexual technique.